WANDERINGS IN
PATAGONIA

AN INDIAN CAMP

Travellers, Explorers & Pioneers

WANDERINGS IN PATAGONIA

OR
LIFE AMONG THE OSTRICH HUNTERS

JULIUS BEERBOHM

NONSUCH

First published 1879
Copyright © in this edition 2005
Nonsuch Publishing Ltd

Nonsuch Publishing Limited
The Mill, Brimscombe Port,
Stroud, Gloucestershire, GL5 2QG
www.nonsuch-publishing.com

British Library Cataloguing in Publication Data.
A catalogue record for this book is available from the British Library.

1-84588-062-5

Typesetting and origination by Nonsuch Publishing Limited
Printed in Great Britain by Oaklands Book Services Limited

CONTENTS

INTRODUCTION TO THE
MODERN EDITION

It seemed like an unfinished portion of the globe, the very skeleton
of a landscape. The outlines were there, indeed, the framework of the
intended structure. There were bold hills, sheltered valleys, isolated
peaks, deep basins; but over all was silence and desolation, all was
empty and void.

So appeared Patagonia to the tired and disconsolate traveller Julius Beerbohm, in
the throes of his despair. The phosphorous plains and basalt flats rose up before him,
and the wind swept coldly across the Santa Cruz River; the warm sun had vanished
behind the towering Andes. What food had been available to Beerbohm and his
companions, the fleet-footed guanaco and the fretful rhea, was now nowhere to
be seen. One might forgive the author's capriciousness in such stern conditions,
one might understand how he might come to see this various and verdant land as
simply 'the last of nature's works.' Over the course of his journey, from the port
of St Julian to the troubled haven of Sandy Point, his opinion of this spectacular
landscape and its worth would change as rapidly as that landscape itself.

In August 1877, Beerbohm's voyage across this wild land began. Patagonia,
nestled between Argentina and Chile, possessed of volcanoes and glaciers, deep
lush valleys and barren steppes, had long held an enchantment for the curious
and intrepid. In 1520, Antonio Pigafetta, the Italian navigator aboard Magellan's
historic voyage, reported seeing 'giants' upon these shores, a claim which travelled
swiftly around the world. It was given credence by numerous reports which
followed; the crew of the *Dolphin*, under Commodore John Byron, perhaps took
a little poetic license in their sightings of men some nine-feet tall; Antoine Knivet,

who sailed with Sir Thomas Cavendish, would not be outdone, and described seeing the bodies of men no less than twelve feet in length. These otherworldly creatures were the native Teheulche Indians, and were undoubtedly of impressive stature. The name 'Patagonia', from the Spanish for 'big feet', remains as tribute to this. The details of their giant-like form were, however, like the reports of Mark Twain's demise, somewhat exaggerated.

The Teheulche people were, in fact, an intelligent and cultivated people. It was in their company that George C. Musters famously spent time, as recounted in his wonderful *At Home with the Patagonians*. This work is widely held as one of the most comprehensive ethnographic documents of these people, and was also a source of inspiration for Beerbohm in undertaking this voyage, as he himself describes:

> I was extremely glad of the opportunity thus afforded me of making the acquaintance of these wandering tribes, for whom, having read Captain Musters' *At Home with the Patagonians*, I had always felt a particular interest. Captain Musters adopted the only plan by which it is possible to gain a thorough insight into the peculiarities of the morality and customs of such people, and to discover the principles which guide their dealings amongst each other and amongst strangers . . . living amongst them as one of them, sharing their pleasures and hardships, and doing his duty in the hunting-field or in the ballroom with as much zest and earnestness as if he intended passing his whole existence among them . . .

Another examination of the Teheulche culture exists in the form of Auguste Guinnard's *Three Years Slavery Among the Patagonians*. While circumstances did perhaps dictate that this author's account would not be quite as empathetic as Musters', it does give ready testimony to the complexity of this social group, and provides another source by which a deeper understanding might be gained.

Together with the complex social hierarchies and codes of interaction which are revealed in this work, and those of Guinnard and Musters among others, an awareness of the spectacular environment in which the Teheulche exist is paramount. The deer-like guanaco abounded, who were gifted by nature with 'the head of a camel, the body of a deer, the wool of a sheep and the neigh of a horse'. Less common, though equally as palatable, were the armadillos, the *zorro*, or Brazilian fox, the great wild stallions, and the pumas. Beerbohm describes his first memorable encounter with a puma as follows:

I had heard a great deal of the cowardice of these animals, how you may go up close to them and strike them dead with the bolas, without their offering any resistance; but still this particular puma, I reflected, might happen to be an exception to the general rule, and turn out to be an unpleasantly brave animal, which might possibly resent being fired at . . .

And, of course, there were the ostriches, who lend their name to the title of this volume. The hunting of these animals was in truth a spectacular pursuit, for which reason alone it warrants its elevated status. The flightless birds were chased on horseback by the natives, the skilful and the author. They were remarkably fast, and should their pursuer manage to get within striking distance, he would then attempt to fell his foe by means of bolas, two stones or rocks strung together. To attempt such a task on horseback over ever fickle ground was undoubtedly a sight to behold. The ostriches alone might disagree, though in fact, they were not ostriches at all but rheas, including the *rhea darwinii*, and only a distant cousin.

Patagonia, its people, and the wildlife on which they rely are, however, only part of Beerbohm's fascinating tale. Wanderings in Patagonia is just as much about the author's own development, a very personal struggle against what seem at times to be insurmountable odds. The fact that this story unfolds against one of the most spectacular backdrops which nature can provide is simply the best of fortune.

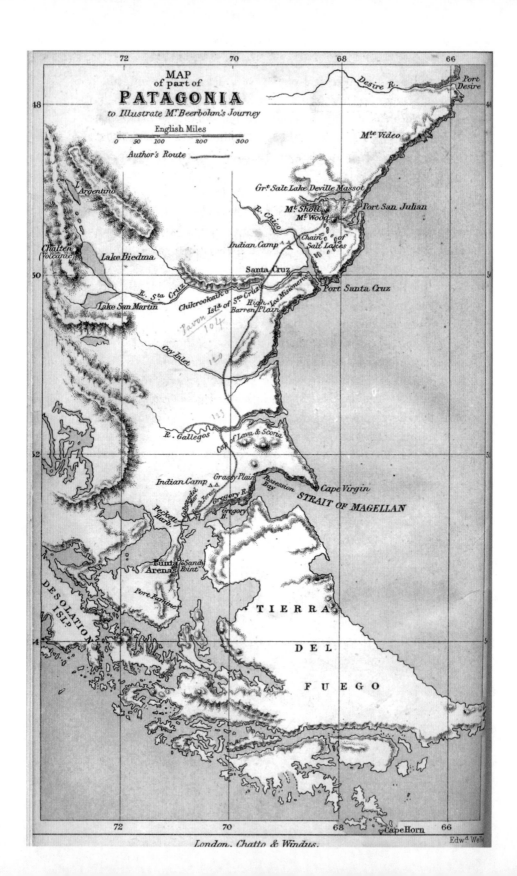

MAP
of part of
PATAGONIA
to Illustrate Mr Beerbohm's Journey

English Miles

0   50   100   200   300

Author's Route ———

Desire R.   Port Desire

Mte Video

Gr. Salt Lake Deville Massot

L. Argentino

R. Chico

Mt Sholl
Mt Wood   Port San Julian

Chalten (Volcano)   Lake Biedma

Indian Camp ^ ^   Chain of Salt Lakes

Santa Cruz

R. Sta Cruz

Chirrookaik   Port Santa Cruz

Lake San Martin   Isla of Sta Cruz   Los Misioneros
                                 High Barren Plain

104

Coy Inlet   120

R. Gallegos   Cor. of Lava & Scoria

Grassy Plain   Possession Bay

Indian Camp ^ ^   Cape Virgin

Gregory R.   STRAIT OF MAGELLAN
Peckett Harb.   Gregory B.

Punta Sandy Point
Arenas

Port Famine

DESOLATION ISLD.

T I E R R A

D E L

F U E G O

Cape Horn

London, Chatto & Windus.

Edwd Wells

I

ARRIVAL IN PATAGONIA

IN the month of August, 1877, I found myself on board ship, bound from Buenos Ayres for the coast of Patagonia, in company with a party of engineers, who were going to survey that portion of the country which lies between Port Desire and Santa Cruz.

After leaving the River Plate we encountered adverse winds and heavy weather, which kept us tossing about for three weeks, without making any material progress on our course. At last we got a fair wind, however, which soon brought us close to our destination, the port of St. Julian (lat. 49° 20′ S.); and one morning, together with my five-o'clock coffee, the cabin-boy brought me the welcome news that land was in sight. I jumped out of bed and ran on deck, careless of the hail and rain which were falling in blinding showers, and of the wind which blew off the land, far colder and sharper than we had hitherto experienced. On looking to leeward I could at first see nothing but a thick bank of clouds; but presently the horizon got clearer, and I descried a dark, lowering line of coast, of fierce and inhospitable aspect, rising abruptly from the sea to a considerable height.

I had not long to examine it, for a sudden shift of the wind shrouded the whole coast in mist, and it did not become visible again till the afternoon, when the weather cleared up, and the sun shone out brightly. The wind, however, slowly increased in violence; by the time St. Julian came in sight we were plunging along under reefed topsails, and the captain began to think that we should have to stand off the port till the force of the storm had abated,—a prospect which threw us all into dismay, as we had already been looking forward with vivid expectations to the pleasure of stretching our legs on *terra firma* the next morning,—a luxury which those who have made a long sea voyage can fully appreciate.

While the captain was yet doubtful what course to take, the matter was summarily decided by the weather itself. The wind, which had hitherto been blowing from the north-east, shifted to the south-east, and redoubled its fury; and rather than run the risk of standing off the port for the night, under a lee shore and with a strong current setting in to the land, the captain elected to face the lesser danger, and enter the port.

The necessary orders were accordingly given; a man was sent aloft to look out for banks or rocks, and all preparations were made for any emergency. An anxious time ensued for all on board, as we steered slowly in under the northern headland of St. Julian, menaced on either side by steep and rugged cliffs, falling vertically down to the water's edge; the sea dashing at their base with an angry roar, and hurling the white spray almost to their very summits. The gale howled through the rigging, and a thousand sea-birds, startled at such an unusual apparition, circled round the ship, white and silent, seeming to eye us with an unpleasant curiosity.

Suddenly we heard a shout, "Breakers ahead!" and every one turned pale and looked anxiously forward. Right in front of us, and forming a belt across the entrance of the port, stretched a line of breakers, boiling and foaming like a cauldron; while to the left a long ledge of black, jagged rocks pierced through the waters, promising certain destruction, should we drift upon them. For a moment the captain was irresolute; but it was too late to go back; in any attempt to put the ship round we should have gone on the rocks, and there was, therefore, no alternative but to continue our course and dash through the breakers, leaving the rest to fate. On we went, with beating hearts and strained nerves, as the threatening roar of the foaming rollers became louder and louder. In another second we were in their midst, and every one held his breath in suspense. Suddenly there was a shock; the ship quivered, and I was thrown violently on my face. By the time I got to my feet again, all danger was over. We had crossed the harbour bar, and were now sailing slowly up the bay, in comparatively smooth water, and congratulating ourselves on our escape from what had looked a most serious peril. The wind, too, had lulled, and by the time we let go the anchor all was still and calm. The sun was just setting; one by one the gulls, albatrosses, and other sea-birds, which had hitherto been continuously sweeping round the ship, disappeared; and not a sound was heard from either side of the broad bay.

On arriving in port, after a long sea voyage, the sudden change of scene and associations, the bustle and noise of commercial activity steamers, lighters, and other small craft, plying from shore to shore, the ships moored alongside the wharves, taking in or discharging cargo, the busy hum arising from the distant town, the sight of new faces, and the sound of strange voices—all combine to excite and bewilder one, contrasting forcibly with the dull, quiet, and drowsy sameness of the life one has just been leading during several weeks of dreary navigation.

But none of these accustomed sights and sounds gladdened our hearts in the desert harbour where we had just safely come to anchor, after our stormy passage. The silence of death reigned everywhere, and its mysterious effect, joined to the wild character of the surrounding country, whose bold, bare hills were now looming gigantic and black in the gathering dusk, impressed me with a vague sense of awe and wonder.

And not out of harmony with the gloomy spirit of solitude which broods over St. Julian are the tragic memories connected with the three famous nautical expeditions which have visited its inhospitable shores.

We were anchored between two islands—Justice and Execution Islands. These names were given to them by Sir Francis Drake, who visited St. Julian in 1578. On the former he caused one of his party, a Master Doughty, to be put to death for alleged insubordination. Sir Francis found a gibbet already erected on one of these islands, which had been left there by Magellan, who passed the winter of 1520 at St. Julian, and who, during his stay, had also to quell a formidable mutiny which broke out amongst his little fleet; and which, but for his timely energy, foresight, and courage, might have ended fatally for him. The ringleaders were executed. In more modern times, another fatality occurred during the expedition of the *Adventure and Beagle*, 1832. A Lieutenant Sholl, a young officer of much promise, died there, and was buried on a point overlooking the bay which now bears his name. The spot is marked by a small cairn, bearing an inscription recording the date, etc.

As I looked over the bay, for all the change that has happened there since, either in the rugged outlines of its shores or in the spirit of silence and desolation that hangs over them, it seemed that it might have been but yesterday that Magellan dropped anchor there, with his quaint, high-pooped craft,—

"The first who ever burst into that silent sea."

Peering into the darkness till a mist rose into my eyes, I gradually fell into a half-dreaming, half-waking state, and presently I seemed to behold some strangely rigged vessels, lying close to me in the bay. Magellan's own ships! There was the tall, spare figure of the intrepid commander himself, standing on the poop of the largest vessel, dressed in a brown leather jerkin the cross-hilted sword at his side; and I could plainly mark the expression of dauntless enterprise on his weather-worn brow, and the determined gleam of his sharp grey eyes, whose glance now wandered over the far shore, and now rested reverentially on the high cross fixed on the poop. I could see the quaintly costumed sailors busy at work on deck, repairing rigging, mending boats, or making sails, talking and shouting the while in a strange tongue. Hardy, noble figures these men, who, in the frailest of craft, braved a thousand dangers in the wildest countries, and fearlessly carried the symbol of their religion to lands which mariners of to-day, with all the advantages of modern instruments and superior vessels, approach with the utmost mistrust and dread. Soon a bell rang, and all was silence; the men left their work and gathered round the commander, who, I thought, seemed to be addressing them. And then floating over the waters came the sound of the "Ave Maria!" weirdly sweet and plaintive.

But at this juncture somebody shook me, and I woke up, to find it was all a dream, and to remember that Magellan had been dead and buried for centuries, and that I, a son of the nineteenth century, had come to that spot, not to plant the true Cross, but to find what the country was capable of—and that, finally, it was time for supper.

II

EXPLORING THE INTERIOR

THE next morning we were up betimes. The weather was fine, and, as there was no wind, not too cold, though the taller hills were covered with snow, and the thermometer stood considerably below zero. Plenty of sea-birds were flying round the ship, or disporting themselves in the water, heedless of our presence; but on shore there were no signs of animal life stirring anywhere. Preparations were made for getting the horses on shore as quickly as possible, as their long confinement was beginning to tell injuriously upon them. In the mean time a boat was lowered; and taking our guns, a few of us started off for the shore, to find some suitable spot to land the horses, and to have a general look round.

A short pull brought us in sight of a little cove, with a strip of sandy beach leading up to the mainland, which fell steeply down on all sides, so as to form a kind of natural corral, where the horses would be quite safe, and conveniently sheltered from the wind. There we accordingly landed, roughly waking the echoes, which had doubtless been comfortably sleeping for many a long day, with a loud hurrah, as we jumped on shore and climbed up the bluff which shut in the cove. There the first object which met our sight was the little cairn already mentioned, commemorative of Lieutenant Sholl. It was standing, probably, just as it had been left by the hands which reared it, as the Indians seldom, if ever, come so near to the port. The letters of the inscription were still tolerably visible; for the stones suffer little from the action of the atmosphere, and gather but few mosses or lichens in that dry climate, where, during nine months of the year, hardly any rain falls, and where all vegetation is stunted and scanty.

The view we obtained from our present standpoint was very limited, the horizon being bounded by a chain of conically shaped hills, flattened at the top, and generally similar in outline and height. The country which they enclosed appeared to consist of a series of irregular plains, broken up by glens, or "cañons," as they are aptly called in Spanish, with here and there an isolated hill and an occasional plain of short extent. There were plenty of bushes of a thorny species scattered everywhere, and in the glens the grass seemed to flourish in tolerable luxuriance, though on the higher-lying land it was less plentiful, the ground there being covered with pebbles of porphyry, worn round and smooth by the action of water at some remote period.

After our long cooping up on board, we were not equal to any prolonged exertion, and soon got tired of climbing up the steep hills and escarpments, especially as there was no employment for our guns, either in the shape of beast or fowl. We therefore went back to our boat, to get at which, as the tide had already fallen considerably, we had to wade knee-deep through a long tract of black, slimy mud. As there is a tide-range at St. Julian of from thirty to forty feet, the ebb and flood tides rush in and out with great rapidity, and we often had great difficulty in pulling back to the ship, even with four oars, when the wind and tide happened to be against us.

The rest of that day was employed in getting the horses on shore,—a task which was successfully accomplished before the tide commenced to rise again, so that they had comparatively little distance to swim to the cove. The poor animals seemed as glad as we had been to find themselves on land once more, and testified their satisfaction by neighing and frisking about with great vigour. In the evening we made a short excursion to Justice Island, close alongside of which we were anchored. Whilst exploring it, we startled a large covey of shag, numbering quite a thousand, which, to judge by the accumulation of guano, appeared to roost there habitually. They did not fly up immediately at our approach, but waddled clumsily down to the beach, holding their bodies quite erect, and flapping their wings in a ludicrous manner. The sailors killed several with sticks, and subsequently cooked and ate them, notwithstanding the strong fishy taste of the flesh.

Early the next morning, together with two of my companions, I started on an expedition towards the interior, with a view to discover what kind of country lay beyond the range of hills which bordered the horizon. We took some provisions with us, as we did not expect to be home till the evening, thinking it prudent not to rely on our guns for our dinner, after the experience of the previous day of the absolute absence of game; indeed, we left them behind us, as being rather irksome on horseback.

Mounting the three freshest horses we could find amongst our stock, we struck off at an inspiriting gallop. We had not gone far, however, before it came to an abrupt ending. The plain over which we were riding suddenly terminated, descending into a deep ravine, which seemed to wind from the hills down to the port. The descent was rather steep, but we got down somehow; and then our horses had a hard climb up the opposite side, rendered still more arduous by the loose nature of the pebbly soil, which afforded no reliable hold, giving way under their feet. On reaching the top, we found ourselves on another plain, intersected a little further on by a ravine similar to the one we had just crossed; and so we continued, now scrambling up and down these canons, now leisurely trotting over short plains, whose level surfaces gave our horses time to get breath and to prepare for tackling the next ravine, until gradually we got nearer to the hills, beyond which we hoped to meet some more pleasant variety of landscape.

Presently we came to a very broad cañon, on the surface of which we observed some irregularities, which, on inspection, proved to be the remains of some human habitation. Portions of wall, about three feet high, were still standing, and here and there lay several pieces of timber, but, excepting a millstone, half embedded in the soil, there were no other vestiges of those who had once attempted to create a homestead in this lone spot.

The colony, on the site of which we were now standing, was founded in 1780 by Antonio Viedma, under commission from the Viceroy of the River Plate Provinces, and was abandoned in 1784, in accordance with a royal order, chiefly on account of the sterility of the soil, which rendered agriculture impossible. The colonists also suffered severely from scurvy, and were further troubled by the Indians, whose hostility they seem to have incurred. The Spaniards, whatever grave faults they may have committed in the administration of their South American possessions, developed great energy and spared no expense in their endeavours to colonize Patagonia, and numerous expeditions were despatched from Buenos Ayres with this object. Settlements were established at Port Desire and other spots on the coast, all of which, sooner or later, came to share the fate of the colony of St. Julian.

And indeed it is not to be wondered at. Unless some very cheap manure be discovered, by means of which sand may be profitably fertilized, or unless some new source of riches at present hidden be discovered there, it is much to be apprehended that Southern Patagonia is destined to remain almost entirely unpopulated and uncultivated till the end of time. In the cañons, where there is a little alluvial soil, some scanty crops might be harvested, or a patch of potatoes might be cultivated; but the spring and summer months are so dry, that even these limited attempts at husbandry might not always be attended with favourable results. Sheep might be reared in the valley of the Santa Cruz River, though not in great numbers, as the pasturage there is rather limited, and the grass itself is coarse and long, and not particularly adapted for sheep, for which it is preferable that it should be short and fine.

The coast is extremely rich in fish, however, and a dried-fish trade might, perhaps, be successfully carried on with the Brazils, where a good market exists for this article, which forms the staple diet of the poorer classes in that country. An attempt to start an industry of this kind was made by a Frenchman, M. E. Rouquand, who established himself, in 1872, at Santa Cruz, with all the machinery, boats, etc., necessary for such an undertaking, under a concession granted to him by the Argentine Government. He built several houses and sheds there, the materials for which were conveyed at great expense from Buenos Ayres; and when everything was ready, and he was about to go practically to work, a Chilian man-of-war steamed into Santa Cruz one day and signified to him that he was trespassing on Chilian territory, and would be required to leave immediately. Chili, it appears, claims jurisdiction over Patagonia as far as Santa Cruz River, and could therefore not permit any one to attempt to benefit that country whose authorization to do so came from the Argentine Government. The latter country does not admit Chili's claims to possession over the territory in question, but contented itself in this case with a diplomatic protest against the act of violence committed in defiance of the Argentine flag, under whose protection M. Rouquand had laid out his capital and his energies. In the mean time M. Rouquand is of course ruined, as neither Government has granted him any compensation for the losses he has sustained by his arbitrary ejection. After such an example, and as the settlement of the territory dispute seems to have been indefinitely shelved by the easy-going countries concerned, it is easy to understand why no one has hitherto been found disposed to risk his time and capital in an endeavour to establish any industry on the Patagonian coast.

Turning our backs on the "Glen of the Spaniards," as it is still called in Indian traditional nomenclature, we again continued our journey towards the hills, which were in reality much further than they had appeared at first sight, being, by the rather roundabout road by which we had come, about fifteen miles from the port. Another hour's ride brought us to their base, and as the keen morning air had made us all rather hungry, before going any further we dismounted, and having made a good fire with the branches of some of the thorny bushes which abounded everywhere, and which proved an excellent combustible, we discussed a hearty breakfast of cold meat and biscuit.

After a short rest we remounted and rode slowly up a glen which led between the hills, craning our necks expectantly as we climbed the escarpment which bounded its further end, from the top of which we should have a good view of the surrounding country. We emerged on the summit, and behold, there was nothing but an immense plain, stretching away in dreary uniformity to the far horizon. The scene was not a cheerful one. Down in the cañons the grass is long and green, and clumps of underwood, growing at intervals, lend a pleasant variety to the landscape. But on the plains, which often extend uninterruptedly for thirty or forty miles, all is different, and nothing more dull and dreary can be imagined than the view presented by these immense tracts of land, where, by reason of the sterility of the soil and the fierce winds which sweep continuously over them, no vegetation can possibly flourish. The soil is sandy and covered with stones, with here and there an isolated tuft of grass, withered and grey, whilst a peculiar gloom is further added to the character of the scene by the sombre, melancholy hue of a straggling, stunted bush, the jume, which grows there in considerable quantities,—in its blackness and ugliness, the fit offspring of such an uncongenial soil.

The plain we were now standing on was no exception to the general rule, and we found but little inducement to remain immersed in a long contemplation of its charms; so, turning our horses' heads, we followed the course of the hill range, which trended in a semicircle towards the port. After having ridden for some distance, the plain terminated, and we descended into a broken country again, marked with the usual peculiarities of glen and plateau. We presently came in sight of a large lake, which we thought might contain fresh water but on coming closer we found that the shores were covered with salt crystals, and that the soil in the vicinity was impregnated with salt too. The lake measured about two leagues long, by a league and a half broad at the widest part, but the water was very shallow everywhere. We could see a herd of guanacos standing in the centre, and the water did not reach to above their knees. I have frequently observed these animals standing in the salt lakes which abound everywhere in Patagonia, but whether they actually go to drink, I am not prepared to say, though it is hard to account in any other way for their presence there. We looked with some curiosity at these guanacos, as they were the first animals we had met with as yet on the mainland, but they were too far off for us to be able to observe them with accuracy. I shall describe the species at another opportunity.

In the mean time it was getting late, and our horses, which had been severely tried by the nature of the ground we had gone over that day, were beginning to show signs of fatigue. My horse, in particular, was completely done up, and it was with great difficulty that I managed to keep up with my companions.

At sunset we were still a long way from the ship. Dusk came on apace; the hills around us first grew indistinct and hazy, and then gradually settled down into a dark, solid mass, blackly defined upon the lighter background of the sky, over which the stars were now glittering in the frosty air. It was getting cold, too, and I began heartily to wish myself on board, especially as every moment it became more apparent that my horse was in imminent peril of collapsing altogether.

Still he stumbled on, occasionally shying wildly at the glimmering whiteness of some heap of bleached guanaco bones, or startled at the fanciful shapes assumed by the bushes in the deepening shadows of night.

Presently, as I was riding up a rather steep escarpment, my horse's saddle-girths slipped back, the saddle rolled over, and I fell with a heavy thud to the ground. The moment he felt relieved of my weight, and before I could jump up and seize the reins, the horse turned round and leisurely trotted back to a glen we had just left, where there was some fine grass, which had evidently taken his fancy in passing. I ran after him as fast as I could, but he gently, though firmly, refused to be caught, pausing now and then, whenever he had distanced me, to snatch a few mouthfuls of grass, and then starting off again as soon as I came near to him. This kind of thing went on for a long time, and when I had at last caught him, and had picked up the various saddle-belongings I was completely done up. Not more so, however, than the horse, for when I remounted him he refused to budge an inch, and at the first touch of the whip, quietly lay down. I was now in a pleasant plight. I shouted, in the hope that my companions would hear me, but no answer came. They had evidently not noticed my mishap, and had continued their route, thinking I was coming up behind.

Reluctantly I had to make up my mind to stop where I was till the morning, though the prospect was anything but cheerful. I was too tired to go on foot, and no persuasion would induce my horse to stir. I was very hungry, and, unfortunately, one of my companions carried what remained of the meat and biscuit; and though it was extremely cold, I had no other coverings for the night but my saddle-cloths, having neglected to bring my fur robes with me. Luckily, I had a box of matches; and having broken off a sufficient quantity of dry branches from the bushes, I soon managed to have a good fire burning, whose warm glow afforded me no little comfort. As a substitute for supper, though it was not a satisfactory equivalent, I smoked a pipe, and then, wrapping myself up as well as I could in the saddle-cloths, I lay down by the fire and tried to go to sleep. This I could not accomplish; for although I fell into a half-doze at first, as soon as the fire got low, the cold thoroughly woke me again, and I had to set off and look for a fresh supply of firewood,—by no means a plentiful article. I soon made the fire burn up again; but, do what I would, I could not get to sleep, and finally had to abandon the attempt as hopeless.

The night seemed interminable. Occasionally I would get up, and walk to and fro to pass away the time quicker, but the cold soon drove me back to the fire. I confess I should have liked some companion to enliven my weary vigil. All alone in the wild desert, surrounded by the dark night, I felt quite an uncanny feeling come over me as I listened to the strange whisperings which seemed to creep through the grass and hover in the air, as the wind rose and swept down the narrow glen where I was camping. The more I listened, the more these noises seemed to multiply, till at last there was quite a Babel of confused sounds and vague murmurings. Now and then I would start to my feet, fancying I heard voices close to me, or something would rustle mysteriously past, and a sound as of faint laughter would seem to ring from out the depths of the darkness around me. For a time I was kept in quite a state of nervous agitation; but it gradually wore off, and soon I became stolidly indifferent to everything except the fire, to replenish which from time to time I had to make an excursion in search of wood.

The hours went slowly by, as I sat watching the stars creeping over the heavens, longing wearily for daybreak. At last, worn out with fatigue, I fell into a troubled slumber, and when I opened my eyes again the sky was already grey with dawn. My fire had gone out, and my limbs were stiff with cold. On a bush near where I was lying four carranchos, a kind of hawk, were perched, eyeing me with a complacent, watchful look, as if they expected shortly to make a meal of me. Feeling quite uncomfortable under their unholy gaze, I flung a stone at them; but they merely flew up a little, circled once or twice round me, and then lighted again on another bush, as much as to say, "Never mind; we can wait." They abound in the pampas, and assemble in great numbers whenever a puma slays a guanaco, as the former often contents itself with merely sucking the blood of its victim, leaving the rest to these birds and the vultures, who soon pick the bones clean.

I rekindled the fire, and after I had warmed my stiffened fingers I saddled the horse, which I had tethered to a bush during the night, and rode off towards the port. I arrived at the cove after about an hour's sharp riding, and found that my companions had also been obliged to pass the night in the open air, as their horses had eventually succumbed, under the fatigue consequent on their hard day's work.

III

THE OSTRICH HUNTERS

DURING the next few weeks we were busy examining the country in the vicinity of St. Julian, without finding anything of special interest to reward our pains. Near the salt lake alluded to in the last chapter we discovered some extensive deposits of phosphate of lime, but as they are very far from the port, they must be considered to have practically no commercial value. Perhaps, however, when all the guanos and nitrates of more accessible regions have been exhausted, the phosphates of Patagonia may be utilized for manuring purposes, but in the interests of agriculture it is to be hoped that that day is as yet far distant.

St. Julian is a far superior harbour to either Chubut or Port Desire, but there is a dearth of fresh water in its vicinity during the months from October to June, which is of course a great drawback, and neutralizes its other advantages. Indeed, the whole country is but sparsely watered. South of the Rio Negro, which must be considered as the dividing line between Patagonia and the Argentine Provinces, there are only small rivers, the Chubut, the Desire, and the Santa Cruz. Coy Inlet and Gallegos rivers during nine months of the year are unimportant streams, and the former at certain periods frequently dries up altogether.

The river Chubut has never been followed to its source by any trustworthy traveller, but Dr. Moreno, an Argentine explorer, from personal observations and from information obtained from the natives, is inclined to place its source as taken from a lake, called Coluguapé by the Indians, which lies somewhere between lat. 44° to 45° S., and long. 68° to 69° W., Greenwich. Thence it flows in a north-north-easterly direction till within about sixty miles from its mouth, and then, having received near this point the waters of several small streams from the Cordilleras, it flows from west to east, and finally empties itself into the Atlantic in lat. 42° 20′ S. The depth of the river at forty miles from its mouth varies from five to eight feet, according to the time of the year. Its current is not so rapid as that of most Patagonian rivers, but its extremely tortuous course makes it difficult to navigate. Its estuary forms a tolerably safe harbour for craft of light draught.

The Welsh colony at Chubut which numbers at present about 700 souls, was founded by the Argentine Government in 1865. It is not, and never has been, in a flourishing state; but this is due not so much to the unfertility of the Chubut valley as to the fact that most of the people sent out from Wales by the Government agent to form the proposed agricultural colony were miners, who of course knew nothing about farming matters. For a great many years the colonists were supported entirely by the Government, and on several occasions when accidents had happened to the vessels which were bringing stores for them from Buenos Ayres, they were saved from starvation by the Indians, who supplied them with guanaco and ostrich meat. At present the prospects of the colony are rather more hopeful: about 15,000 bushels of wheat were harvested last year; but even now the colony is not self-supporting, and costs the Argentine Government large sums annually for provisions and other assistance afforded the colonists.

South of Chubut lies Port Desire, formed by the estuary of the river, or rather stream, of that name. The Desire does not rise in spring and summer, like Gallegos and the other Patagonian rivers, to any great extent—a circumstance which makes it probable that it does not take its source in the Cordilleras, but rather from a chain of hills, which, according to Dr. Moreno, traverses the centre of Patagonia, running south-south-west from the Sierra de San Antonio, near the Gulf of San Matias. The Spaniards formed a colony at Port Desire, which, after having existed for a few years, was officially abandoned in 1807. The remains of a fort and some houses are still standing near the port, as well as some apple and cherry trees, with which the climate of Patagonia seems to agree very well.

I pass over the incidents of the rest of my sojourn at St. Julian, as having no relevancy to the object of this work. Suffice it to say that by the little Government schooner which makes two or three voyages annually from Buenos Ayres to the Rio Negro and Santa Cruz, and which on this occasion put into St. Julian to bring us our correspondence, I received some letters, conveying important news, which made my speedy return to Buenos Ayres imperative. About the same time a party of ostrich-hunters, attracted by the smoke of our fires, came to St. Julian from Santa Cruz, partly out of curiosity to see the unusual visitors, and partly to trade for biscuits and tobacco. They did not stop long; and as they were going back to Santa Cruz, and from there to Sandy Point in the Straits of Magellan, where I should be able to take a steamer for Buenos Ayres, I embraced this favourable opportunity, and, packing up a few things, started off with my new acquaintances.

We had not gone far, however, when it commenced to rain, and there being no particular object in getting wet, we halted for the day, and took shelter under our tent, hoping that by the next morning it would be fine again. In this hope we were disappointed; it rained incessantly for about four days, during which we of course remained where we were, and very tired I soon got of it. The ground was as damp as could be, and so loosened by the moisture that the stakes of our tent gradually gave, and the slack canvas being no longer water-tight, little pools of water gathered round the furs and saddle-cloths which served us in lieu of bedding, permeating them with a general dampness, which made our nightly slumbers rather uncomfortable. The daytime we passed cowering round the fire, with some covering thrown over our backs to keep off the rain, the front part of the body requiring no extra covering, for as fast as it was wetted it dried by the fire, which for this purpose was allowed to assume formidable dimensions. Under such unfavourable circumstances, conversation rather flagged, as may be imagined, being limited to occasional prophecies and conjectures as to when the weather might be expected to change for the better. But in revenge, the tobacco-pipe and the maté-pot went round the circle without any intermission, and during the days of forced inaction consequent on the rain, we consumed startling quantities of those two almost indispensable commodities of pampa life.

Yerba-maté is a kind of tea in great repute throughout South America, especially amongst the country people, who drink it at all their meals, and whenever they have nothing particularly to do, which is very often. It is the leaf of a shrub (*Ilex Paraguanensis*) extensively cultivated in Paraguay and the Brazils, constituting, in fact, the chief article of commerce of the former country. The powdered leaf is steeped in boiling water and imbibed through a thin pipe (*bombilla*), perforated with holes, so as to prevent the fine herb from being sucked up with the fluid. It has a bitter, aromatic flavour, and though usually taken with sugar, many find it equally palatable without the latter adjunct. Its restorative powers are marvellous, and frequently, when thoroughly exhausted after a hard day's ride, I have taken a cup or two of maté, and found myself immediately revived and invigorated. It is decidedly a better stimulant than either tea or coffee, and as it does not seem to lose its flavour by exposure to the air and damp as quickly as those articles do, it is naturally preferred by those whose profession forces them to take these qualities into account in the selection of their victuals. Maté, as I have already said, is indispensable to the hunter in Patagonia. For months it is often the only addition he can make to his otherwise exclusively meat diet. In fact, he is never without it, except when in the saddest plight, and for its sake he would forego any other luxury, such as sugar, biscuit, or rice.

It is surprising that hitherto no attempt has been made to introduce yerba-maté into Europe as an article of domestic consumption. It has only to be known to be appreciated, and as it could be imported *pure*, far cheaper than tea or coffee, it might in time prove a formidable rival to those beverages, especially among the working classes, to whom its invigorating qualities would particularly recommend it.

Whilst the rain is pouring down upon us, I may as well take the opportunity of introducing my four companions to the reader. But first a few words as to their common profession, that of the ostrich hunter.

In the plains that stretch from lat. 40° to 53° S., and from the sea-coast to the Cordilleras, the ostrich and the guanaco roam in immense numbers, their procreativeness being such as to more than neutralize the ravages caused among them by their numerous enemies, such as the Indians, the pumas, and the foxes. The Patagonian ostrich is much smaller than his African cousin, and the feathers are not nearly so valuable, the price usually paid for them at Sandy Point being from $1 to $2 per lb. The trade of the ostrich-hunter is not, therefore, very lucrative; but his wants, on the other hand, are very modest. Besides, he follows his profession more from a love of the wild pampa life, with its freedom from irksome restraint and awkward social obligations, than from any desire to amass wealth; more from a necessity to satisfy his vagabond instincts, than from any impulse derived from some definite aim in life. His hunting-ground extends as far as he chooses to gallop. His stock-in-trade consists of ten or twelve hardy horses, five or six dogs of a mongrel grey-hound species, a lasso, a pair of bolas, a knife, a revolver, and a long steel; besides, of course, all the necessary accoutrements for his horse, which, together with the indispensable capa, form his bed at night.

The capa is a long robe of guanaco furs, about five and a half feet long, by four and a half broad. They are made by the Indian women, who are very clever at sewing, notwithstanding the primitive clumsiness of their rude tools. Their needles consist of pieces of bone sharpened to the requisite point, and the thread they use is made from guanaco sinews. The skins are of the young guanacos before they are three weeks old, as after that time the fur becomes coarse and woolly. These capas are extremely warm, and effectually protect one from the cold winds that blow over the pampas, when almost any other garment would prove insufficient. A novice experiences considerable difficulty in the management of their somewhat awkward folds, especially on horseback; but the Indians wear them with infinite ease and grace.

The bolas, or balls, are of two kinds, being either two round stones or pieces of lead, covered with leather and joined by a thong of from six to eight feet long; or three balls, united by thongs to a common centre. The latter are used chiefly for guanaco and not a little skill is required to handle them efficiently. After having been swung round the head till the requisite pitch of velocity has been attained, the balls are hurled at the animal pursued and becoming firmly twisted round what ever part of its body they may fall on, they effectually hamper its speed, and enable the hunter to come up to it and give the *coup de grace* with his long knife.

With no other *impedimenta* than the above-mentioned, the ostrich-hunter roams at will over the vast pampas. At night-time he makes himself at home under shelter of some thick bush, which, if such be his caprice, may become his head-quarters for weeks and even months, especially if the game in the vicinity be abundant. His movements are altogether uncertain, and by no means regulated by any reference to time, to the course of which he is sublimely indifferent. The chase supplies all his wants. With the hide of the guanaco he makes his lasso, reins, bolas, and even shoes; whilst its flesh, varied by that of the ostrich, forms his staple article of diet. When he has collected a sufficient quantity of feathers, he pays a flying visit to Sandy Point, sells them, and with the produce lays in a new stock of tobacco and maté, renews his wardrobe, *i.e.* say a shirt, a poncho, a jacket, and a chiripà; and if there still remains anything over, he may buy another horse, or some dog which may have taken his fancy.

For the rest, he is a careless, easy-going vagabond, always cheerful, whatever plight he may be in, and submitting with calm philosophy to any of the many hardships the inclemency of the climate may entail upon him. There are, however, few ostrich-hunters *pur sang* in Southern Patagonia, though up near the Rio Negro they are more numerous; but those one does meet with are all distinguished by the characteristics I have described.

I will now attempt a sketch of my four companions, beginning with the most striking among them, Isidoro, who is several times mentioned in Captain Musters' interesting book, "At Home with the Patagonians." He was an Argentine Gaucho, with a dash of Indian blood in his veins, who had come down to Patagonia many years ago from the Rio Negro. He was a slender, well-built man, with a pleasant, swarthy face, of a warm, earth-brown complexion, set in by a profusion of long black hair, which he carefully groomed every morning with a comb, whose teeth being old, were decayed and few and far between, kept for the purpose in the recesses of a rather greasy cap. Broad and shaggy eye-brows, meeting over a bold Roman nose, and shading a pair of bright, restless eyes, habitually veiled by half-closed lids and the longest of lashes; slightly high cheek-bones; full, thick lips; and a shaggy beard and moustache, completed the *tout ensemble* of his really striking face, the general expression of which was one of intelligence and good humour.

His dress, which combined materials of Indian as well as European manufacture, was not unpicturesque, and consisted of a woollen shirt and a "chiripà"—a covering for the lower limbs something like a kilt, secured by a strap at the waist, into which were stuck the inevitable hunting-knife, revolver, pipe, and tobacco-pouch—while his feet were encased in potro boots, tied at the knees with Indian-worked garters; and over all hung the long capa.

The recipe for making a pair of potro boots is very simple, and the operation requires no previous knowledge of the cobbler's art. Having killed your horse, you make an incision with a sharp knife round the hide above the hock, say at the commencement of the lower thigh, and another a couple of inches below the curb-place, and then proceed to draw the hide off the legs. Each leg will thus supply a comfortable wellington, in which the point of the hock has become the heel. Of course, before fit for wear, the hide must be well softened by hand,—a task which requires no little patience, for if not thoroughly done the boots after a time will become quite hard and useless. As soon as they have been worn long enough to have taken the shape of the foot, the toe-ends are sewn up, and the transformation of your horse's hocks into easy-fitting boots is an accomplished feat.

When hunting, the belt and bolas are strapped outside the capa, so that the upper part of the latter may fly loose whenever any exertion requires that the arms should be free, as when lassoing or throwing the bolas.

Isidoro was one of the best riders I have ever seen, and even amongst the Indians he was allowed to have no equal. The most unruly colt became quiet in his hands, and after a few ineffectual attempts to dislodge its rider, would sullenly acknowledge the mastery of his firm hand and easy seat. All his horses were wonders of tameness and careful and intelligent teaching. His method of taming them I subsequently had an opportunity of studying, and in due course will revert to it. He was equally proficient in the use of the lasso and bolas, seldom, if ever, missing his aim. One of his peculiarities was his extreme watchfulness; not the slightest detail could escape his vigilance; and when any one, as often happened, would mislay a knife or some such object, to save further trouble, Isidoro was always appealed to as to its whereabouts, which he would invariably point out immediately,—the missing article often lying under a bush or saddle-cloth, where it had been thrown by its careless owner perhaps a day or two ago. It seemed as if Isidoro made it his special duty to look after every one's things, though, to judge by appearances, he never paid particular attention to anything except his pipe, which seldom left his mouth. His sharpness of vision was intense, and he could detect guanacos and ostriches on the far horizon, when I could see nothing but bushes or clouds. Another distinguishing feature was his taciturnity. Only on very rare occasions have I heard him utter more than three or four words at a breath, and often he would sit for hours with the rest of us round the fire, listening attentively to all that was said, without breathing a syllable the whole evening. As the owner of some thirty fine horses, he was considered quite a rich man amongst the Indians and ostrich-hunters; and, on account of his honesty, good nature, and quiet, unassuming bearing, he was a favourite with every one.

We will pass on to Garcia, who, in appearance at least, formed a striking contrast to Isidoro. His yellow beard, brown hair, and blue eyes seemed to betoken a Saxon rather than a Spanish descent. However, be that as it may, he was a true Gaucho, and but slightly inferior to Isidoro in horsemanship and general address as a hunter. He had formerly been a soldier on the Argentine frontiers, and in that capacity had had many a fight with the Indians, thrilling accounts of which he would often favour us with over the evening's fire. Subsequently he had worked as "tropero" (cattle-driver) on the Rio Negro, a profession which in due course he had relinquished in order to become an ostrich-hunter. Having lived more amongst civilized people, his manners were less abrupt than Isidoro's, and he was rather more talkative and genial than the latter.

Next comes Guillaume, who was by birth a Frenchman, and who had originally been a blacksmith; but some chance having wafted him to Patagonia, he had taken a fancy to the country and remained there, and was now fast becoming naturalized. He was an active, intelligent fellow, and equal to any amount of hard work. One of his most striking features was his enormous appetite, the amount he could devour at one meal being simply astounding. It is on record amongst his companions that he demolished a whole side of a young guanaco at a sitting. But notwithstanding this extraordinary faculty for eating, he was as thin as could be, and always had a hungry, half-starved look.

His very antithesis was Maximo, the last of the group, who in size and corpulence might have competed with the most Herculean Patagonian Indian. He was an Austrian, age twenty, I think, and had formerly been a sailor, but having been wrecked on the syren shores of Patagonia, like Guillaume he had been unable to withstand its subtle attractions, and having embraced the profession of ostrich-hunting, with the natural aptness of sailors, he had soon mastered the mysteries of his craft, and was already an adept in the use of lasso and bolas. His strength was such as his burly dimensions warranted, and he would often surprise us by the ease with which he would tear up firmly seated roots and stout underwood for firing purposes. He was, moreover, as I was surprised to find, an accomplished linguist, and spoke Spanish, Italian, French, German, and English with tolerable fluency, though I think he could neither read nor write. His appetite, like Guillaume's, was Homeric, the two being a host in themselves.

Maximo was not so rich as his companions; indeed, his whole property consisted in a horse and a dog. The former was a wiry little animal, and apparently impervious to fatigue; for its owner was by no means a feather-weight, and it was a matter of continued astonishment to me, how it managed to carry him along, day after day, over tiring hilly country, with occasional fierce gallops after ostriches, without ever showing signs of distress. Neither was his attire so elegant or so comfortable as that of his companions. It consisted, on my first becoming acquainted with him, of a shirt and a pair of trousers; boots he had none, but would now and then wear a pair of sabots, made with the skin of the hind legs of the guanaco. However, the capa made up for all defects in dress, and Maximo was perfectly content with things as they were. Withal he was the best-tempered fellow imaginable, and the stoic indifference he showed to the discomforts of rain and cold, and his equanimity under all circumstances, were simply heroic.

As these four men, who by various strange chances had been thrown together on this desert spot, from such different parts of the world, were to become my companions during a long period of hardship and adventure, I have described them at some length, especially as I feel sure that their peculiar and utterly unconventional mode of life, so different from that of the ordinary people one meets in everyday intercourse with the world, will invest them, in the eyes of my readers, with the same romantic interest with which I regarded them.

IV

THE FIRST HUNT

THE rain continued to pour down almost without interruption for four days, till one afternoon a shift of the wind brought a definite change for the better; the clouds cleared off, the sun shone out brightly, and we were cheered by the sight of blue sky again.

We hastened to spread our furs, sheepskins, and general clothing on the bushes to dry, as everything had got more or less damp during the recent downpour, and, thanks to the wind and sun, by supper-time we were able to indulge in dry shirts and stockings again, which, with the luxury of having dry beds to creep into that night, in perspective, sent up our spirits a hundred degrees, and made the conversation over that evening's supper as lively as it had hitherto been dull.

Maximo told the story of the shipwreck which had first thrown him on Patagonian shores; Garcia related some exciting incident of his frontier warfare experience; Guillaume recounted the hardships and dangers he had undergone during the siege of Belfort in 1870, having belonged to the brave garrison which defended that fortress; and even Isidoro, yielding to the genial influence of the moment, so far abandoned his accustomed silence as to tell us how, when a soldier in the Argentine service at Rio Negro, he had deserted and run away with a tribe of Tehuelche Indians, who were going south, with whom he lived for a long time, and from amongst whose brown-skinned daughters he had eventually taken unto him a wife. He admitted, however, that his matrimonial existence had not been a happy one. Mrs. Isidoro, it appears, took to drinking, and became too noisy and violent for her husband, who of all things loved quiet; so without any further fuss, and without many words, as was his custom, he led her back to her father's tent, where, with a short explanation, he left her, thus consummating his divorce *a mensâ et thoro* with expeditious ease, and securing for himself the blessing of undisturbed peace for the future.

We rose at daybreak the next morning, and commenced preparations for starting. The horses, some fifty in number, were driven together, those selected for the day's work were severally lassoed, and this being done, the others were allowed to disperse again and return to their grazing, whilst we got ready.

Although as tame as cats in every other respect, very few of these Indian-tamed horses allow one to approach them on foot; as a rule they can only be caught with the lasso. When a horse observes that it has been singled out from the herd for capture, it does its utmost to evade the flying noose, and often gives a great deal of trouble before it can be finally caught; but the moment it feels the lasso alight round its neck, it will stop short in the fiercest gallop, and immediately gives up any attempt at resistance, which it knows would be useless; and when once it is bridled, the lasso may be removed, and it will stand in the same spot for hours, without attempting even to graze.

Our stock of provisions, viz. some rice, biscuit, farina, sugar, maté, and a stone bottle of gin, were carefully packed up, and together with the tent and cooking utensils, an iron pot, a saucepan, and a tin kettle, were placed on the pack-horse, a sturdy animal, who trotted away under his load as if it had been a feather-weight.

We then commenced saddling our own horses,—a somewhat lengthy operation. The articles which constitute the saddle-gear of a horse in the pampas are rather numerous, and at night-time serve, with the aid of the capa, as mattress, bed-clothes, and bedstead. First one lays two or three blankets or cloths, folded square, on the horse's back, taking care that they lie smooth and form no creases; over these comes a covering of leather, called a "carona," which consists of two thick pieces of leather sewn together, and which is very useful at night-time, as it forms a damp-proof foundation for one's bed. On the carona the saddle is placed, and firmly secured to the horse by means of a broad leather girth, and over the saddle again are laid the sheepskins, furs, or whatever coverings one may possess. All being ready for starting, we strapped our capas well around us, a few logs were heaped on the smouldering fire, we warmed our hands, which had got stiffened with the cold whilst saddling, smoked a last pipe, and after a look round to see if anything had been forgotten, jumped into the saddle, whistled to the dogs, and we were off, *en route* for Santa Cruz.

It was a bright morning. The wind was just cold enough to make one feel grateful for the warm sunshine, and to give that exciting tingle to the blood which influences one's spirits like a subtle wine. I felt its power, and a strange elation made my pulse beat quicker, as I rode gaily along, inspirited by the strong, springy step of the good horse I bestrode, and inhaling deep draughts of the pure clear air, which seemed to sweep the cobwebs of care from my brain, and to blow all unpleasant thoughts far from me, making me feel gloriously happy in the mere consciousness of the fact that I breathed and had being.

I seemed to be leaving the old world I had hitherto known behind me, with its turmoils and cares and weary sameness, and to be riding merrily into some new sphere of free, fresh existence. I felt that without a pang I could break with old associations, renounce old ties, the pomps and the pleasures, the comforts, the bothers, the annoyances of civilization, and become as those with whom I was now travelling,—beings with no thought for the morrow, and therefore with no uneasiness for it either, living the life of our nomadic ancestors, in continual and intimate contact with nature,—an unchequered, untroubled existence, as wild, simple, and free as that of the deer that browse on the plains.

We were riding along a broad glen, down the middle of which a rapid stream was flowing. Guillaume and Maximo were busy driving the horses before them,—no easy matter, as, now and then, one or two would lag behind to crop up a mouthful of grass, or the whole troop would make a dash in the wrong direction, only to be got together again after much galloping and shouting.

The neighing of the horses, the continual cries of "Jegua! Jegua!" with which they were urged along, and the tinkling of the bells on the "madrinas" (bell-mares), broke cheerfully on the silence of the glen, and startled many a flock of wild geese, who were disporting themselves there in numbers; and occasionally a guanaco or two, who had been grazing in the young grass, would gaze at us in a momentary fit of curiosity, and then bound away with their graceful, springy gallop, neighing defiance at us as they glided swiftly up the far ravine.

After we had gone some way, Isidoro and Garcia and myself rode ahead of the horses, in order to look out for ostriches, Isidoro taking one side of the cañada, which was about a mile and a half broad, and Garcia and myself the other. I felt very excited, as it was my first hunt after this kind of game. The dogs, with erect and quivering tails, and noses down, were eagerly running this way and that, scenting the ground, or snuffing the wind which came in light puffs down the cañada.

OSTRICH-HUNTING

Presently they made a simultaneous dash forward, and started off after something, and my horse, evidently an old hunter, with a sudden start that almost threw me out of the saddle, dashed after them, *ventre à terre*, like wildfire, side by side with Garcia, who was already loosening the bolas to prepare for action.

I soon descried the ostrich, which was hurrying along as fast as its legs would carry it, wings drooping and neck outstretched, with the whole covey of dogs close on its heels. The race was at first doubtful, but a moment of indecision brought the ostrich into difficulties, and the dogs slowly gained on their prey. Already the foremost one was up to it, when the ostrich suddenly darted sideways, whilst the hounds, unable to stop their impetuous speed, shot forward a long way before they could recover themselves. By that time the bird was half-way up the side of the glen, and out of danger; and Garcia whistled to the dogs, who came back slowly and sulkily, with their tails between their legs, looking wistfully over their shoulders at the retreating bird, which was already a mere speck on the summit of the ravine.

Garcia told me that the ostrich, like the hare, often resorts to this trick of "doubling" when hard pressed. It is not always as successful as it had been in the present case, as the dogs generally know the exact moment and in what direction the ostrich is going to double, and are prepared accordingly.

We were riding slowly along, talking about our late disappointment, when another ostrich started up almost from under our very feet. With a wild shout we dashed after it, Garcia getting ready with the bolas, now our sole means of capturing the bird, as the dogs had lagged far behind us on some wrong scent. The horses were on their mettle, and in headlong chase we tore after the distressed quarry; but though we strained every nerve, we could not gain an inch of ground, and in another second we should have lost the ostrich, who was making for the steep ravine-side, when Garcia, swinging the bolas two or three times round his head, flung them with strong hand at the retreating bird. Luckily lighting on its neck, they entangled its legs, and it fell to the ground, kicking desperately. An instant after and we were up to it, and Garcia ended its struggles by breaking its neck, and then proceeded to disembowel it,—a process watched with peculiar interest by the dogs, the offal, etc., being their share of the spoils.

The trophy was then hung to Garcia's saddle, and we went back on our tracks to look for the nest; for, from the bird having started up so close to us, Garcia surmised that it must have been sitting, as during that period they are loth to leave their nests, at the approach of danger, till the very last moment. Garcia proved to be right, for, after a short search, we came upon the nest, which contained fourteen eggs,—a prize we were not long in securing to our saddles.

I found the nest to be of the roughest description, being simply a hole scooped in the ground, under shelter of a bush, and made soft for the young chicks by a few wisps of grass.

The number of eggs found in a nest varies from ten to forty, being usually about twenty. In size, the Patagonian ostrich's egg is equal to about eight hen's eggs. It is the male bird that hatches the eggs and looks after the young,—being, I believe, the only male among birds which does so. The period of incubation is from twenty to twenty-four days. During rainy weather, he never leaves the nest, but will sit for six or seven days without feeding. In fine weather, he grazes for an hour or two in the evening, but never strays far from the nest, as Master Reynard, who is always prowling near, would soon make a raid on the eggs. It is said that if one egg is broken or abstracted from the nest during the absence of the male bird, on returning he will immediately detect the theft, and become so furious that he will dash the remaining eggs to pieces, and dance round the nest as if frantic.

After the hatching period, the birds lay their eggs promiscuously about the plains. These eggs are called "huatchos" by the natives. They keep for a long time, and I have frequently met with huatchos in April, which, although they must have been laid more than six months at that time, were still fairly eatable.

The ostrich of Southern Patagonia (*Rhea Darwinii*) is smaller than the "Avestruz moro" (*Rhea Americana*), as the species which frequents the country near the River Negro is called by the natives. The colour of its plumage is brown, the feathers being tipped with white, whereas the moro, as its name indicates, is uniformly grey. The *R.Darwinii* are extremely shy birds, and as their vision is remarkably acute, it is by no means an easy matter to catch them, unless one has very swift dogs to hunt with.

At the approach of danger the ostrich often crouches flat on the ground, with its neck stretched out under the grass, remaining motionless in this position till the dogs have gone past. This stratagem is successful when the wind is blowing against the scent; but when the contrary is the case, the dogs soon discover the hiding bird, which, doubtless too bewildered by the sudden failure of its naively artless ruse, makes no attempt to escape.

Our companions by this time were a long way ahead of us, so we started after them at a brisk gallop. On the way we met Isidoro, who had also been fortunate, as two ostriches dangling from each side of his saddle evinced.

We continued to journey along the winding ravine, all helping now to drive the horses, and keep them well together,—an essential matter when rapid progress is desirable, for if the troop once gets broken up and scattered, one may spend no end of time in galloping about and herding the horses together again.

At about five o'clock we passed a fine thick bush, of considerable height, which appeared so well adapted for affording shelter that we resolved to camp under it for the night, especially as I, not being accustomed lately to such long rides, already began to feel rather tired and shaken.

In a few minutes after we had made this decision, our horses were unsaddled, the saddle-gear, packs, ostriches, etc., thrown higgledy-piggledy in a heap, and every one lay down in the grass to stretch his limbs and smoke a pipe,—a simple indulgence which, under such circumstances, becomes an absolutely priceless luxury.

A small fire was then made, the kettle filled from the rivulet which ran down the centre of the ravine, and as soon as the water boiled, maté was prepared, and we sat for some time silently imbibing that stimulating concoction, whose wonderful powers of banishing fatigue I have already alluded to.

Presently Maximo and Guillaume went off to collect firewood, whilst Isidoro and Garcia busied themselves with plucking the ostriches and laying

the feathers in bundles, in which form they enter the market. I stretched myself out on my furs and awaited the dinner-hour with eager expectation, as my ride and that sharp, dry air peculiar to Patagonia, had given me the real pampa appetite, under the influence of which one becomes so inordinately and irksomely ravenous, and experiences such an unnatural craving for food, as quite to justify one in considering one's self attacked by some transitory but acute disease, which has to be undergone by the stranger in Patagonia, like those acclimatizing fevers peculiar to some tropical countries.

In an hour or so Guillaume and Maximo returned, bringing a huge bundle of dry wood between them, and the kitchen being Maximo's special department, he immediately set about getting dinner ready. Thanks to his efforts, a fine fire was soon blazing; the big iron pot was filled with water, ostrich meat, and rice, and set to boil, and several other dainties were set to roast on wooden spits or broiled in the ashes, emitting odours of grateful promise as they sputtered and browned under Maximo's delicate handling.

Meanwhile, we sharpened our knives, took up comfortable positions round the fire, and the *chef* having declared everything ready, the onslaught commenced.

I append the *carte* for the benefit of those curious in such matters:—

> *Pot-au-feu* (rice, ostrich meat, etc.).
> Broiled ostrich wings.
> Ostrich steak.
> Cold guanaco head.
> Roast ostrich gizzard, *à l'Indienne*.
> Ostrich eggs.
> Custard (ostrich eggs, sugar, gin).

A glance at the above will show that a pampa dinner may be pleasantly varied. Of the items mentioned, I think the ostrich wings are the greatest delicacy, tasting something like turkey, and, as I then thought at least, perhaps even finer. The ostrich gizzard, too, was worthy of note, being broiled Indian fashion, with hot stones,—a task which, as requiring great care was superintended by Isidoro himself, who in his way was a remarkable cook. The flavour of ostrich meat generally is not unpleasant, especially when fat. It varies greatly, according to what part of the bird it is from. The wings, breast, and extremity of the back are the tit-bits. The thighs are coarser, and bear a close resemblance to horseflesh.

When all the meat was consumed, Isidoro, who, by-the-by, seemed to be able to produce anything that was required from somewhere or other (generally from his cap, which was quite a storehouse for all kinds of extraneous articles), now turned up with a small soup plate and a dilapidated spoon, and I was requested to help myself to the broth and rice in the pot, handing the plate back to Isidoro when I had finished, who in his turn passed it to Garcia, and so on till it had gone round the circle.

We then lay back to smoke and recover from our exertions, whilst the dogs cleared up whatever fragments remained from the feast.

Here I may say a few words about the dogs, of which there were in all about eighteen with us. Most of them were greyhounds of more or less pure breeds, imported by the Welsh settlers at Chubut; the others being nondescript curs of heavier build, which were useful for pulling down the guanacos brought to bay by the fleeter but less powerful greyhounds. Their various merits and failings formed the usual topic of an evening's conversation, their owners comparing notes as to their respective achievements during the day's hunting, or recalling previous wonderful performances worthy of remembrance.

We were quite overrun by such a number of dogs, and often they became a nuisance only to be borne when we remembered that after all they were the meat givers, without whom we should find ourselves in a very unpleasant plight. They had a peculiarly happy knack, when wet, of creeping into one's furs, and making one's bed damp for the night; and often I have been awakened by one of them trying to go comfortably to sleep on the pillow beside me, and thrusting its cold nose into my face as a preliminary. When eating, if I happened to lay down a piece of meat for a moment, it was sure to be immediately snapped up by one of them, and they would even snatch away the morsel held in my hand, if I did not take care to keep them at a safe distance. All provisions had to be put on the top of a bush, well out of their reach, as neglect in this particular might bring on the unpleasant alternative of going supperless to bed.

We sat for some time round the fire, chatting and smoking, and then each looked out for his furs and bed-gear, arranged his couch, and before long we were all fast asleep.

I woke once, roused by some horse which had strayed from its companions, and which was snuffing at me curiously, till on my starting up it bounded away, snorting with terror.

Before going to sleep again I looked around me. There was a faint scent of fresh earth on the cold night air, and a slight frost had fallen over bush and grass, which told that dawn was not far distant. The moon was shining full over the valley, bathing it in hazy light. I could see the horses standing about in black knots of twos and threes, some dozing, some grazing, the bells of the madrinas occasionally breaking the deep silence with a soft tinkle. Round the fire, some logs of which still smouldered redly, my companions lay motionless, sleeping soundly under cover of their warm furs.

Fascinated by the strange novelty of the scene and the calm silence of the hour, I lay for a long time gazing about me. I watched the soft charm of silvery indistinctness, lent to the landscape by the moon's rays glittering on the frosty crystals, gradually fade away, as the moon's splendour paled before the new light which sprang up in the east. Soon the bushes, the grass, and the winding ravine stood out sharply defined, looking grey and bleak in the sober light of dawn. The face of nature seemed blank and wan, like the face of a man on whom the morning light streams after a night of vigil. With a shiver I drew my head under my capa, and fell into a sound sleep again.

V

JOURNEY TO THE RIO CHICO

WHEN I awoke there was a good fire crackling and blazing cheerfully, and I lost no time in getting up and joining my companions, who had already risen, and were taking maté and enjoying the warm glow of the fire, which at that damp, chilly hour was indeed welcome.

As we were not going far that day, we were in no hurry to start off, preferring to wait till the sun should get high enough to dispel the cold mist which hung over the country.

We took our ease over breakfast, therefore, and it was already nearly midday when Maximo rode down the ravine to collect the horses. We waited for a long time, but to our surprise he did not re-appear; and presently Garcia went after him to see what was the matter. After a time they both returned, driving the horses before them, but reporting Isidoro's stallion and several of his mares missing. From the appearance of the tracks, Garcia seemed to think that some wild stallion had made a raid on the mares and driven them off,—a piece of news which filled Isidoro with consternation, as he feared that by that time the missing animals might be forty or fifty miles away, beyond any hope of recapture. Without losing any time, therefore, we all saddled, and leaving some of our gear and packages under the bush where we had been camping, we started off on the trail.

Some way down the cañon we came to a place where there had evidently been a fierce struggle. The ground was torn up in all directions, and Isidoro's sharp eye was not long in detecting some tufts of hair lying in the grass, which he declared came from the coat of his own bay stallion. Some of the hoof-marks were very large, larger than could have been made by any of his horses, and he quite confirmed Garcia's surmise, that some "bagual" (wild horse) had carried off the mares, after having previously fought and vanquished his own stallion. We had no difficulty in following the trail, as the recent rain had made the ground quite soft. The tracks went along the cañon for some distance, and then suddenly turned and went up the cañon-side on to the plain. We had not gone far over the latter when our horses pricked up their ears and began to sniff the air in a nervous manner. A few strides more brought us to the edge of the plain, and in the cañon at our feet we discovered Isidoro's bay stallion, looking very crestfallen and woe-begone. At our approach, he gave a faint neigh of satisfaction; but he had hardly done so, when it was answered by a triumphant pæan from another quarter, and from behind a bend in the cañon, meekly followed by Isidoro's mares, issued a magnificent black stallion. Undeterred by our presence, he made straight for his but recently vanquished rival, with head erect, nostrils distended, and his long mane and tail streaming in the wind. As for the bay,

"Not a moment stopped or stayed he;"

but ignominiously took to his heels, and started up the cañon at full speed.

Isidoro, who was some way ahead of us, galloped to the rescue. The bagual, strange to say, however, suddenly rushed at him, standing up on its hind legs, and beating the air with its fore feet in a threatening manner. Taken by surprise, Isidoro had hardly time to loosen his bolas when the furious brute was upon him, and for a moment I thought it was a bad case. But Isidoro was as cool as he was adroit, and in another second the bagual dropped on its knees, half stunned, struck full in the forehead by a well-aimed blow of the balls. Before it could recover, Garcia's lasso whizzed through the air and lighted on its neck, and then, setting spurs to his horse, he galloped away at full speed in an opposite direction. The shock, as the lasso tautened, threw his horse on its haunches, but the stallion lay half strangled and powerless. To finish matters, Maximo whipped his lasso over its fore feet, and drew them tight together, and the poor brute was thus reduced to utter helplessness.

We could now contemplate it at our ease. It was a splendidly made animal, and far larger than any of the horses of our troop. I was very much astonished at the way it had shown fight, as I had imagined that, being wild, it would have fled at the sight of man. I pleaded strongly that its life might be spared, but the fact that it was in very good condition weakened the force of any argument I might bring in support of my plea, fat meat in spring being a luxury which my companions did not feel justified in depriving themselves of, if fate chanced to throw it in their way. The poor bagual was accordingly despatched, skinned, and cut up, but eventually none of the meat was eaten, for, much to every one's disappointment, it proved so strong that even the dogs did not care to touch it.

We now returned towards our camp. The bay stallion, his wrongs avenged and his abducted wives restored to his affectionate keeping, kept neighing and tossing up his heels in a state of high glee, without, to all appearance, being troubled by any misgivings as to whether his recent ignominious defeat had caused him to forfeit the esteem of his family circle.

On our way back Isidoro told me that he had frequently seen troops of wild horses near St. Julian, and that at times the Indians make excursions to those regions on purpose to catch them. At the foot of the Cordilleras there is a smaller, and in every way inferior breed of baguals, several tame specimens of which I subsequently saw amongst the horses of the Southern Tehuelches.

Having reached the camp, we loaded the pack-horse and resumed our journey southwards. We continued to follow the windings of the ravine for some distance, and then, turning abruptly, we rode up one of its steep sides and found ourselves on a broad plain, which seemed to stretch away interminably, presenting the characteristics of dreary gloom and hopeless sterility I have already described.

The wind, which down in the ravine we had scarcely felt, blew with astonishing violence upon the plain; the gusts were so strong occasionally, that we could hardly keep our saddles, and at intervals we encountered squalls of hailstones of unusual size, which, coming full in our faces, caused us no little annoyance. It was bitterly cold, too, and I was thankful for my capa, which kept me tolerably warm, though I had great difficulty in keeping it tightly folded round me, for if the wind could but find hold in the smallest, crevice, it would blow the capa right off me. In fact, it requires a peculiar knack, only to be attained by long experience, to enable one to wear a capa on horseback with ease and comfort.

Conversation under the adverse circumstances was not very practicable, and we rode on for the most part in silence. It was altogether a miserable day, and that tedious plain seemed as if it were never going to end.

We reached its limit rather suddenly, however. I had been holding my head down for some time, to avoid a passing squall of hailstones, and so had fallen insensibly to the rear of my companions. On looking up presently, I found, to my astonishment, that they had vanished as if by magic, and I was apparently alone in the plain.

I galloped forward, and their sudden disappearance was soon explained, for in a couple of minutes I found myself at the edge of the plain, which terminated abruptly, descending almost vertically into another plateau, which lay some two hundred feet below, down towards which my companions were slowly winding their way in a zigzag line, as the descent was too sharp for them to ride straight down. I had considerable difficulty in following them, as the violence of the wind seemed doubled at this spot, and it was only by clinging firmly to the neck of my horse that I prevented myself being blown from the saddle. In a measure as I descended, however, the wind grew less boisterous, and on arriving below it entirely ceased. I soon rejoined my companions, and presently, on coming to a spring of fresh water, with some good pasture near it for the horses, we resolved to go no further that day.

We accordingly unsaddled and made the usual arrangements for the night, which, as the sky looked rather threatening, on this occasion included setting up the tent. This precautionary measure was a wise one, as towards morning there was a slight fall of snow, and when I woke up I found the whole landscape whitened over.

Garcia and the others were of opinion that we had better remain where we were for the day, as they considered that travelling through the snow might be bad for the horses; so, there being nothing better for us to do, we crept under our furs and went to sleep again till about midday, by which time the snow had nearly all melted away under the influence of the sun, which shone out brightly. Isidoro and Garcia then rode off hunting. Maximo, Guillaume, and I, being lazily inclined, remained by the fire, and beguiled an hour or so with breakfast.

Afterwards they went to fetch firewood, whilst I amused myself by practising with the bolas. I found it very difficult to use them with any precision; in fact, they always took exactly the opposite direction to that in which I wished to throw them, and finally, in an attempt to "bolear" a bush, I very narrowly missed poor Maximo, who was just coming up behind me.

As an instance of the skill which may be acquired in the use of the bolas, I have several times seen Isidoro throw them at some refractory colt, at full gallop, with such true aim as to make them alight round its hind legs, and effectually pinion them, without doing the animal any harm whatever,—a feat which requires immense confidence and nerve, as the bolas, which are very heavy, being generally made of stone or lead, have to be flung with considerable velocity.

The first hunter to return was Garcia. He had killed a female puma, a great prize, as the meat is excellent, and especially esteemed during the winter and spring months, when it is always fat, whereas the ostriches and guanacos are at that time generally miserably lean. The brute looked very fierce and dangerous; the half-opened jaws displayed a row of cruel white teeth, which gave its face an uncomfortable expression of rage and spite. The fur was of a yellowish grey; and the length of the animal from tip to tail was about nine feet.

The puma abounds in the pampas, where it preys on the guanacos and ostriches, lying in ambush for them in the ravines near where they are in the habit of going to drink. With one blow of its huge paw, it can kill a full-sized guanaco; but, notwithstanding its great strength, the Patagonian puma is of very cowardly instincts, and if attacked by man, quietly receives its death-blow from the balls without any attempt at self-defence. If taken young they can be easily tamed, and in that state their manners closely resemble those of the domestic cat. They are very fond of being taken notice of, and will purr and stretch themselves under a caressing hand, like any old tabby. They are extremely playful and good-tempered, attaching themselves with docility to those with whom they are familiar.

I was travelling in a steamer once, on board of which there was a young puma about two months old, which was being sent to the Zoological Gardens. It was a graceful, affectionate little animal, and became a great favourite during the voyage, relieving many a tedious hour with its playful gambols. Its great delight was to lie hidden behind a spar, and then suddenly spring out on some unwary passer-by, to whose leg it would tenaciously cling, until some other object attracted its attention. Its inseparable companion was a little Scotch terrier, with which it would play for hours together, rather roughly sometimes, it is true, but still without ever showing any traces of a treacherous or spiteful disposition, though occasionally its temper must have been severely tried, as the dog would often seize and carry away its dinner,—a fighting matter with much better-disposed animals than pumas.

At dinner that evening we ate a side of the puma Garcia had killed. After I had overcome the repugnance I at first felt at eating the flesh of a beast of prey, I found the meat excellent, tasting, as I thought, something like veal.

We started early the next morning, as we had a long journey before us, being anxious to reach the Rio Chico, a tributary of the Santa Cruz River, before night-time.

At every step the country across which we were now travelling grew more sterile, and after about an hour's ride, we found ourselves in a region of extraordinary barrenness. Not a blade of grass was to be seen anywhere, and even the miserable scrub of the plains could find no nourishment in that bleak tract of salt sand and broken scoriæ. Traces of volcanic action were everywhere apparent. Immense boulders of solid rock were scattered here and there in chaotic confusion, and on some spots sharp ridges of dark porphyry pierced through the soil, towering up in fantastic shapes, gloomy and bare. It seemed like an unfinished portion of the globe, the very skeleton of a landscape. The outlines were there, indeed, the framework of the intended structure. There were bold hills, sheltered valleys, isolated peaks, deep basins; but over all was silence and desolation, all was empty and void. The finishing touch had been withheld,—the last touch which was to have softened and modulated those rugged contours, clothing their barrenness with verdure, filling the dry basins with clear water, and bringing life and gladness to what was now lying in sad and eternal deathliness.

Nature must have made Patagonia last of all her works, and the horn of Plenty, from which an abundance of rich gifts had been poured over the rest of the world, was well-nigh exhausted when that country's turn to be endowed came round. There still remained a little grass seed, however, and this was carefully scattered over the length and breadth of the land. But little alighted on the hills and plains, for the strong pampa winds swept it down into the ravines and gulches, under the shelter of which it took root and flourished, affording nourishment to the ostrich and guanaco, and preserving the springs of fresh water from the scorching rays of the summer's sun.

But one nook had been altogether forgotten during the distribution of the scanty remains of Nature's gifts, and accordingly had been doomed to remain desolate and barren to the end of time, sustaining no vegetable life, and shunned by all living creatures. And through that unfortunate region I was now riding, gloomily oppressed by the spirit of mournful silence and wild solitude which hung over it, whilst my weary gaze sought in vain some token of organic existence to relieve the monotony of lifeless stone and bare sand hillocks.

We rode swiftly, for we all felt the same desire to escape as quickly as possible to more cheering scenes, but several hours elapsed before the sight of an occasional stunted bush or tuft of grey grass showed us we were nearing a less inhospitable region.

Presently we rode past a long chain of salinas, which glittered and sparkled whitely in the sun. They were now partially covered with water, but in summer it evaporates altogether, leaving a crust of salt on the surface of the lake of from two to four inches thick. These salinas are met with all over the pampas, and from afar often deceive the thirsty hunter, in search of fresh water, by the similarity they present to a sheet of the latter, when the sun shines on their white surfaces. In the depression over which we were now riding, I counted a succession of more than fifty salinas, which stretched away as far as I could see towards St. Julian.

I passed one salina which, at a distance, appeared to be covered with rose-coloured plants. On riding nearer, I found this delusion to be occasioned by a flock of flamingos, which were collected there in great numbers, to all appearance in solemn conclave, after the fashion of storks,—a bird which they also resemble in their general build. They let me come close up to them, and then, stretching out their long necks, slowly glided away, alighting again on another salina a little further off. As they flew up, I observed that the wings were black underneath, in fine contrast to the brilliant hues of the rest of their plumage, which is of a bright crimson colour, and very beautiful. One fine, long feather floated through the air to my feet, and I picked it up, intending to keep it, along with other similar trifles, as a relic of my journey. Isidoro, half in joke, half in earnest, said the occurrence might possibly be an omen of ill luck and bloodshed,—a prediction which was subsequently strangely verified, though I laughed at it at the time, and, of course, thought no more about it.

By this time we had got into the ordinary style of country again,—short undulating plains, and ravines with plenty of grass and underwood. Several ostriches were caught there, and three nests were pillaged, yielding in all some forty eggs, which we secured to our saddles and bodies in various ways.

We now approached the limits of the deep basin or depression across which we had been travelling all day, and were faced by an acclivity, similar in height and steepness to the one we had descended the day previous. In scaling this wall I had a slight mishap; the prolonged strain on my saddle caused it to slip back, the girths loosened, the saddle rolled round, and, hampered by my capa, I was thrown violently to the ground, breaking in my fall four eggs which I had previously somewhat imprudently secured inside my shirt. Maximo came to my rescue, and helped me to my feet again. My ribs felt very sore, and I was severely bruised on the head; but I was glad to come off so cheaply, for if the horse had taken fright and run away, entangled as I was in the saddle-gear and with my limbs imprisoned in the folds of the capa, I might have incurred considerable risk of being dragged over the pampa. We readjusted the saddle,

I remounted, and we started off again, reaching the summit of the escarpment without further mishap.

There we found ourselves on another plain, across which we journeyed for some time, but finding that it was too late to reach the Rio Chico that day, we halted for the night, under shelter of a stout bush of unusual size.

We had a novel dish that evening, in the shape of a pair of armadillos, which some one had caught during the day, and which Isidoro had artistically roasted with hot stones.

The species of armadillo which inhabits Patagonia (*Dasypus minutus*) is much smaller than any of the other varieties known in the Brazils, Paraguay, and the northern provinces of Buenos Ayres. It is found in great numbers throughout the pampas north of the Santa Cruz, though south of that river, according to the testimony of the Indians, it has never been met with. Why the limit of their range is thus sharply defined, I am not prepared to say, though the phenomenon may possibly be accounted for by the fact that the temperature on the plains a short distance south of the Santa Cruz River is surprisingly lower than that of the northern plains, the change being far greater than the mere difference in latitude would warrant. The "mulitos," as the Spanish call them, are remarkably good eating, and even in the towns they are considered great delicacies. In autumn they have a layer of fat on their backs, of from two to three inches, on which they have to draw in winter, as they pass that season in a state of torpor, which relieves them of the trouble of looking for food.

Those that we ate on this occasion were rather thin, as in that month, September, they commence to leave their holes; but otherwise the flesh was succulent and tender, and tasted very much like sucking-pig.

The next morning we set out for the Rio Chico. On the way we passed several herds of guanacos, some of which must have numbered more than two hundred head. They seemed very shy, and disappeared at our approach with great rapidity, though now and then, one or two more courageous than the rest, would hang around us, almost within reach of the bolas, frisking about and executing the most comical antics, as if to show their contempt for us, and their confidence in their own superior speed.

This self-reliance is not altogether unjustified; the guanacos which roam about singly, and which show such impertinent audacity, are generally tough old males of immense endurance and speed, and to overtake them the swiftest greyhound would have to do its utmost.

It is different when a herd is being chased, as then each animal tries to push into the middle of the flock, and a general scuffle takes place, which of course considerably lessens the speed of the mass,—a fact of which the dogs are perfectly aware, inasmuch as they will hardly ever take the trouble to chase a single guanaco, unless specially ordered to do so by their masters, whereas if a herd comes in sight it is difficult to keep them from immediately dashing off after them.

The guanaco has been well described by Captain Musters as having the head of a camel, the body of a deer, the wool of a sheep, and the neigh of a horse. The wool is of a reddish yellow, intermixed with white in certain parts of the body. They are scattered in immense numbers all over Patagonia, and one can never ride far without hearing the shrill neighing of the sentinels, which always outflank the main flock to give warning of the approach of danger. The flesh, when fat, is excellent, and closely resembles beef, but at the season I am writing of it is terribly lean and insipid, and affords very little nourishment, the only palatable part being the head, which we generally roasted under the embers, eating it cold.

We travelled along over the usual succession of shingly plain and grassy ravine for some time, without anything occurring to break the tedium of the ride. Presently, however, a little off the direction in which we were going, I noticed a guanaco lying dead, with fifty or more carranchos hovering expectantly over it; and as the most commonplace incident becomes of deep interest to the traveller on the pampas as to the passenger on board a ship, I rode up to have a glance at the dead animal. It must have been just then killed, for I found the body still warm, and the blood was trickling from a deep gash in its neck. I looked round, but I could not see the author of the deed anywhere, though I did not doubt but that he was prowling near, or else the carranchos would already have settled on the carcase. We had plenty of other meat, so I merely cut off its head, tied it to the saddle, and then rode after my companions.

I had not gone far, however, when my horse suddenly stopped, snorting wildly, and quivering in every limb. I soon discovered the cause of its terror. Crouching under a bush, about twenty paces ahead of me, was a large puma, glaring sullenly at me, with its ugly cat-like head resting between its outstretched paws. I urged my horse closer towards it, but the frightened animal would not budge an inch, and, as I was not within range, I was obliged to dismount.

Drawing my revolver, I cautiously approached the puma, till I was within easy distance. I then hesitated, not knowing exactly whether to fire or not. I had heard a great deal of the cowardice of these animals, how you may go close up to them and strike them dead with the bolas, without their offering any resistance; but still, this particular puma, I reflected, might happen to be an exception to the general rule, and turn out to be an unpleasantly brave animal, which might possibly resent being fired at, especially if not dealt a wound instantaneously fatal.

However, I finally plucked up my courage, took steady aim at the head of the motionless beast, and fired. It did not stir; I had missed. I went nearer, and fired again; same result. I began to get excited, and went still nearer to the unaggressive puma, which was now hardly ten paces distant, its eyes gleaming at me with a fixed and stolid stare. I fired once more, and this time I thought the head twitched. At that moment Isidoro, who had heard my shots, came up to see what was the matter, and with him, of course, came his dogs. They no sooner saw the puma than they flew at it, and dragged it from under the bush. The reason it had remained so immovable was immediately explained; the brute was stone dead. On examining it I found that two of my bullets had lodged in its skull, and another had penetrated its chest, my first shot having probably caused instantaneous death. With the help of Isidoro, I took off the skin, which was a very fine one, and leaving the carcase to the carranchos, we galloped off after the rest of the party.

We reached the Rio Chico at about twelve o'clock. The exact site of its source is not known, but according to Indian testimony it comes from an insignificant stream at a very short distance from the spot we were now at. Like all rivers in Patagonia, it flows down a broad valley, which seems to have been in former times the bed of a much broader river than that which at present flows through it. Thus the valley of the Rio Chico is about three miles broad, whilst the river, at the time I am speaking of, rather swollen by recent rains, was only some two hundred yards in width. The valley of the Rio Gallegos is much broader even than that of the Rio Chico, while one can almost jump over the river itself in summer.

On account of the fine pasturage they afford for horses, these valleys are the usual camping-places of the Indians, and we were therefore not surprised to see several of their tents pitched on the other side of the river. I was extremely glad of the opportunity thus afforded me of making the acquaintance of these wandering tribes, for whom, having read Captain Musters' "At Home with the Patagonians," I had always felt a peculiar interest. Captain Musters adopted the only plan by which it is possible to obtain a thorough insight into the peculiarities of the morality and customs of such people, and to discover the principles which guide their dealings amongst each other and towards strangers. For the nonce he forgot that he had ever belonged to civilization, and became to all intents and purposes a Patagonian Indian, living amongst them as one of them, sharing their pleasures and hardships, and doing his duty in the hunting-field or in the ball-room with as much zest and earnestness as if he intended passing his whole existence among them, and finally becoming a candidate for some vacant caciqueship.

By these means he became intimately acquainted with their habits and ways, their domestic life, their virtues and failings, their loves and their hatreds, and was thus enabled thoroughly to understand them, and appreciate many interesting traits in their character which would have escaped a less attentive and less conscientious observer.

When we reached the ford, some doubts were expressed as to whether it was practicable, the river being swollen far beyond its ordinary level. Garcia rode cautiously over first, therefore, and on his arriving safely on the opposite side, none the worse for a little splashing, the rest of us followed, driving the horses in before us. The dogs remained behind, setting up a most dismal yell as they watched us making our way through the water; but finding no one offered to carry them over, they at last took heart and swam after us.

Leaving our horses to graze with those of the Indians, which were scattered about in knots all over the valley, we set off at a gallop towards the encampment, on arriving at which we were soon surrounded by a crowd of dusky aborigines, who, to judge by their incessant smiles and laughter, must have been exceedingly glad to see us.

Our first care was to set up our tent and carefully stow all our traps and saddle-gear away under it, as there are some amongst the Indians whose curiosity prompts them to minutely inspect any article one may be careless enough to leave within their reach, and whose absence of mind is so extreme as to frequently make them forget to restore such articles to their rightful owners.

I was then at liberty to examine the chattering groups which had gathered round us, watching all our doings with the greatest interest, and probably criticizing my civilized appearance with a freedom which, had I understood their language, I might perhaps have thought the reverse of complimentary.

VI

THE TEHUELCHES

THE plains of Patagonia, barren as they are, afford sustenance to a marvellous profusion of animal life, and swarm with countless numbers of ostriches, guanacos, armadillos, pumas, foxes, and skunks. But they are but sparsely peopled by the human race. It may be estimated that the native population of that vast territory which lies between the Rio Negro and the Straits of Magellan barely numbers three thousand souls, and if the mortality among them continues on the same scale as hitherto, it is to be feared that in a comparatively short period they will have disappeared altogether from off the face of the earth, and survive only in memory as a sad illustration of the remorseless law of the non-survival of the unfitted.

But at no period of its existence as an habitable country can Patagonia have been well populated; no people would voluntarily choose it for a permanent abode, as long as they could range unmolested in the more hospitable regions of the north, and such tribes as have from time to time elected to brave its inclement climate have in so doing doubtless only yielded to dire necessity, finding the elements less formidable to encounter than the unceasing hostilities of more powerful tribes. Thus the Tehuelches, as the Indians who at present inhabit the southern plains are called, have in all probability gradually been driven to this extreme corner of their continent by the more warlike but intellectually inferior races of the north, such as the Araucanians, the Pampas, and others, who in their turn, as civilization advances, may perhaps be forced to quit their present rich pasture-grounds and moderate climate, and fly to the

bare plains of Santa Cruz and St. Julian, eventually to encounter the same fate of extermination as that which now hangs over the doomed Tehuelche race.

The Tehuelches are divided into two tribes, the Northern and the Southern. The Northerners are the least numerous, but, on the other hand, they have the advantage of being less "civilized" than their Southern kindred, who, being frequently in contact with the settlers of Sandy Point, have assimilated not a few of the pleasant vices of "*los Christianos,*" as all white men are called by them. The Northerners generally pass the winter at Santa Cruz, and move as summer comes on towards the Cordilleras. The Southerners range over the country between Coy Inlet and the straits, and now and then pay a visit to the settlement at Sandy Point. In customs and language there is no difference between these two tribes, and in speaking of the Tehuelches, I must be understood to be referring indiscriminately to the Northerners and Southerners.

Notwithstanding that the exaggerated accounts of early travellers as to the stature of the Patagonians have frequently been contradicted and disproved, a great many people seem still to be firmly impressed with the idea that the race of giants is not yet extinct, and that it has for its abode that favoured portion of South America which the Spaniards christened Patagonia. The truth is that, as regards height, all that can be said of the Tehuelches is that they are on the average a tall race, varying in stature from, say, five feet ten inches to six feet. Their muscular development and consequent strength, however, are decidedly abnormal, and in that sense, at all events, they cannot be denied to possess one of the most important attributes of giants.

I once witnessed a remarkable feat of strength performed by a Northern Tehuelche of the name of Koloby. He was leading a horse towards the camp by a lasso, when the animal for some reason or other suddenly stopped short, and obstinately refused to stir from the spot. After a few coaxing but ineffectual tugs at the lasso, Koloby gave a short grunt of impatience, and then, taking the lasso over his shoulder, bent forward, seemingly without effort, and dragged the horse by main force for about twenty yards, notwithstanding its determined attempts at resistance.

The Tehuelches are on the whole rather good-looking than otherwise, and the usual expression of their faces is bright and friendly. Their foreheads are rather low but not receding, their noses aquiline, their mouths large and coarse, but their teeth are extremely regular and dazzlingly white. Their hair, which is long and black, is kept from falling over their faces by a fillet tied round the head. They have little hair on the face or body, and even that they eradicate as much as possible, including the eyebrows,—an operation which must cause no little pain. Why they do this, I don't know, except it may be that they consider it improves their appearance, in which case it seems that in its application to the "poor Indian," the saying "*Il faut souffrir pour être beau*" loses none of its truth or point. In addition to this embellishment, some tattoo their arms or chest, but it does not seem to be the general custom.

Their eyes are small and deeply set; the prominence of the cheekbones gives great breadth to their faces. The colour of their skin seems to vary according to the individual, or rather according to the individual's cleanliness, but as far as I could ascertain, it is of a reddish brown, running in some cases more into a yellowish tinge. Their general carriage is extremely graceful and dignified, and their manners towards strangers and one another are polite and deferential, without a trace of servility; in fact, they have a certain well-bred air of restraint, which is quite impressive, and one never feels inclined to treat them with that familiarity which is bred of contempt, or that convenient assumption of superiority which the white man is so apt to display towards "niggers."

I do not wish to incur the charge of attempting to revive the exploded legend of the "noble savage" in favour of the Tehuelche race, but I must say that in general intelligence, gentleness of temper, chastity of conduct, and conscientious behaviour in their social and domestic relations, they are immeasurably superior not only to the other South American indigenous tribes, but also, all their disadvantages being taken into consideration, to the general run of civilized white men. Their natural talents are displayed in a marked manner by the rapidity with which they pick up a new language, and the ease with which they grasp the totally new ideas which the acquiring of a complex foreign tongue must necessarily entail on a race whose original range of thought is of a most limited nature. Amongst the Southern Tehuelches I met several who spoke Spanish with ready ease, notwithstanding that they seldom had opportunities of practising it. There was one Indian, who called himself Captain Johnson, who surprised me very much when I first met him by asking me, with a round British oath, for "a plug of tobacco." Further conversation brought out that many years before he had lived for a few weeks on board an English schooner, and hence his knowledge of the language, which he spoke extremely well, considering that he had of course never had occasion to keep it up since. Guillaume told me several instances of the ease with which the Indians picked up and retained French phrases, which at their request he had repeated to them. To their many other praiseworthy characteristics I shall presently revert.

The dress of the men consists of a chiripà, fastened at the waist by a belt, which is frequently richly embossed with silver. The capa, or mantle of guanaco furs, already described, completes their attire. When on horseback their feet are encased in botas de potro; but for reasons of economy they do not wear them at ordinary times. The women wear a long calico robe beneath the capa, which is fastened at the throat with a silver brooch, or a simple wooden skewer, according to the circumstances of the individual. Potro boots are a luxury reserved for the men. The children, on whom most of the silver ornaments of the family are lavished, wear a capa, like their elders, and on attaining the age of four or five are invested with the dignity of a chiripà.

When the women grow old they become repulsively ugly; but the young girls are by no means ill-favoured, and the looks of even the plainest among them are invariably redeemed by the bright, smiling expression habitual to them. Their hair is worn in plaits, artificially lengthened by means of horsehair; their complexion, when free from paint, is of a ruddy, healthy colour; and their eyes, which are shaded with long black lashes, are soft and clear.

Without going so far as to assert that the *affaires de cœur* of the Tehuelche maidens are always strictly platonic, I must say that, according to my own observations, and the confirming statements of others, the relations between the sexes are uniformly characterized by a strong sense of decency and unimpeachable propriety. Polygamy is admitted on principle; but no man may marry more wives than he can afford to maintain, and there is, therefore, seldom more than one mistress to each household. Marriages *de convenance* are very rare; but, as a matter of form, the bride is purchased from her parents for a certain number of mares, or whatever objects her lover can afford to give. But as the dowry of the girl generally quite compensates for the expense her lover has incurred in obtaining her, the transaction must be considered rather as an exchange of presents than as a mere unsentimental bargain. Out of mere curiosity to learn the technical details of Tehuelche marriage-settlements, I once entered into negotiations with a rich old squaw, for the purpose of contracting matrimony with her daughter, who was a charming girl of about fifteen. The price we finally agreed upon was eight mares, a bag of biscuits, and some sugar, which I was to procure from Sandy Point. The dowry of the daughter consisted in four new guanaco mantles. I held out for five, and on my remaining inflexible on this point, the negotiations fell through.

Husband and wife seem always to get on very well together; indeed, one of the pleasantest traits in the Tehuelche character is the affection with which relations regard one another. The love of the parents towards their offspring is almost morbid in its intensity. Their grief at the decease of an only child frequently manifests itself in the most exaggerated manner. It is not unusual in such cases for the parents to burn all their belongings, kill all their horses, and reduce themselves to a state of utter poverty,—a touching proof of the sincerity and depth of their sorrow, if not of the soundness of their views on practical economy.

Their indulgence towards their children is unlimited. I have never seen a child chidden or remonstrated with, whatever mischievous pranks it may have been up to, and in all their internal arrangements the interest of the baby portion of the community seems to be the first which is consulted. For my part, I must say I by no means shared in the feelings of the elders with regard to their youthful progeny; on the contrary, I always considered the latter as a most unmitigated nuisance. They are dirty and vicious, as mischievous as monkeys, and as thievish as magpies. The "Artful Dodger" would have had to look to his laurels if he had had to enter into competition with a young Tehuelche. Their deftness of hand, as I have many a time experienced to my cost, is remarkable. On one occasion, I rode over to their camp from Santa Cruz, on an English saddle, and as I knew that the stirrup-leathers, which are in great demand for belts on account of the buckles, would prove too great a temptation, I took care not to leave the saddle at all during my short stay, thinking by that means to obviate any danger of losing my cherished stirrup-leathers. But even this precaution proved insufficient. In an unguarded moment, whilst bending over my horse's neck in conversation with an Indian who was sitting on the ground below me, by way of resting myself a little, I incautiously slipped one foot out of its stirrup, and lay at my full length along the horse's back. I was hardly two minutes in that position, but I was two minutes too long. On resuming my seat in the saddle, my foot sought in vain for the stirrup, and on looking down I discovered, to my wrath, that during my momentary inattention the stirrup-leather had quietly been slipped off and made away with. Of course, I immediately dismounted in a great rage, and set to to find the thief. After a fruitless search, I returned to my horse, and, lo and behold, in the mean while, the other stirrup-leather had disappeared! In my precipitate haste, I had quite forgotten that whilst I was looking for its fellow, it might be abstracted as well; and the upshot of the whole affair was that, with many a strong interjectional reference to my own stupidity, I had to ride stirrupless back to Santa Cruz, some fifteen miles away. I had no doubt at the time, and indeed I subsequently discovered, that two youngsters had been the perpetrators of the neat theft.

One would think that under such training, as they grew older, their faults would increase; but just the contrary is the case, and by the time they attain their fifteenth or sixteenth year they abandon their brattish ways, and become "respectable," steady-going members of their community.

The division of labour in a Tehuelche *ménage* is perhaps not strictly equitable, for by far the greater part of the day's work falls on the fair sex. The men go hunting when the larder is low, and occasionally, in a dawdling kind of way, they mend their riding-gear, or make bolas, lassoes, etc.; but they have an insurmountable aversion to anything that looks like hard work. The squaws on the other hand, are busy from morning till night. They are the hewers of wood and the drawers of water, and all the onus of housekeeping, breaking up the camp, arranging the tents—including, of course, the care of the children, the *cuisine*, and so forth—is delegated to them. When not otherwise employed, they sew guanaco capas or weave fillets, and their fingers, at all kinds of work, are as nimble as their tongues, with which latter they keep up an incessant chatter, which, however, does not prevent them from getting through an astonishing amount of work.

Of their religion little is to be said. They recognize a good spirit and a bad spirit (Gualichu); but there is little sincerity or earnestness either in their reverence for the one, or in their fear of the other. According to the caprice of the moment, either of these spirits is most cavalierly treated by them, and the respect they occasionally profess towards them gives way as often as not to indifference, contempt, or anger. The fact is, that with the Tehuelches the prime rule in life is to take every thing as easily as possible, to the exclusion of all other considerations; and, acting on the doctrine of the Epicureans, that it is a man's duty to endeavour to increase to the utmost his pleasures and diminish to the utmost his pains, they are careful not to admit any theories which might possibly disturb their peace of mind. Thus they are strongly averse to the idea of vesting in a supernatural agent the power of interfering in their affairs to any great extent, arguing that such power having once been vested, it might on a contingency be used detrimentally to their own comfort and interests. On the other hand, it could not escape them that very often a most convenient excuse for their peccadilloes was to be found in attributing them to the evil influence of some bad spirit. To avoid the dilemma occasioned by the above conflicting considerations, they accordingly created the Gualichu, a most accommodating devil, who allows himself to be ignored or brought forward, as may best suit the momentary purpose of his clients. The good spirit, for obvious reasons, one hears very little about; the Tehuelche is quite willing to take the credit of his good actions on himself alone.

The office of chief or cacique among them is not altogether a sinecure; but its authority is extremely limited, being exercised merely in such slight matters as the choice of the spot where the tribe is to camp, the route to be followed, and so forth. The Tehuelches are very jealous of their personal liberty; and complete individual equality is the recognized basis of their social and political system. Paraphrasing Wordsworth, I may say in prose, "A rich man is a rich man to them, and he is nothing more." In other words, the fact of one of their number possessing forty or fifty horses more than his fellows, seems to be accepted by them as a simple fact, which excites neither respect for the possessor nor envy of his good fortune. Nor would it for a moment occur to the owner of the forty or fifty horses to fancy himself in any way superior to his poorer brethren. The little credit which wealth, *per se*, commands, saves the Indians from a great many of the repugnant vices of white men, such as avarice, jealousy, servility, etc., and keeps up a healthy, independent feeling among them, which is pleasantly manifested in the politeness and kindliness of their personal intercourse.

They have a peculiar custom, moreover, which is well calculated to preserve the existing state of things. When an Indian dies, however many horses he may possess, they are all killed, and his other belongings are scrupulously burned. Thus, no family can acquire such a preponderance of wealth, as would enable it, in time, to obtain an ascendant influence over and curtail the liberties of the rest of the tribe. Whatever the defects of this system may be, from the political economist's point of view, it seems to be very well adapted to the desires and circumstances of the Tehuelches; and as an instance of how socialistic tendencies may be practically modified to suit certain exceptional conditions of existence, it is perhaps not without some interest.

If required to distinguish the Tehuelche by a single characteristic epithet, I should call him, not the noble, but the happy savage. Far from being saturnine or grave, he is as light-hearted as a child, all mirth and contentment, and wonderfully easily moved to laughter. Life is, indeed, a very pleasant matter for him. Without any exertion on his part being necessary, all his wants are supplied in abundance. He has no onerous daily drudgery to undergo; he has no enemies to fear; he is not driven from his hunting-grounds to starvation and death, like his North American cousins, by the ever-advancing white man. He is seldom visited by sickness, and his life is unusually prolonged. That he has absolutely no troubles I will not affirm, but if he has any he certainly takes them very lightly.

To conclude these few remarks on the Tehuelche race, in reviewing their characteristics it is impossible not to award them a high rank in the list of uncivilized nationalities. To admit that they have many faults, is, after all, merely saying that they are human; but these faults are redeemed by many unusual excellencies They are good-natured, hospitable, and affectionate; their instincts are gentle; violence and ferocity are foreign to their nature; and though not invariably veracious nor strictly honest, if they think you trust them, they will take care not to deceive you. Their one great failing is their addiction to rum, to whose fatal agency the rapid decrease in their numbers, and the consequent fast extinction of their race, must be ascribed.

But to return to my narrative. Our tent having been set up, and all our saddle-gear stowed away, I strolled into the Indian camp, followed by the chattering crowd which had come out to meet us. My curious glances at these children of the desert were certainly repaid with interest; and they subjected my person and belongings to the closest scrutiny. The texture of my coat was carefully examined, and appeared to give rise to a lengthy discussion, which was carried on with more zeal and earnestness than the merits of the subject would seem to warrant, and nothing but a good stare of several minutes' duration at my face seemed to satisfy even the least curious among them.

The camp was composed of five toldos, or tents, each tent containing on the average about twenty-five souls. These toldos are very practically constructed, and, notwithstanding their formidable size, they are set up or taken down by the squaws in a surprisingly short space of time. A covering made of guanaco skins is drawn over a rough framework of wood, consisting of a double row of stakes and cross-beams, lashed together with thongs of guanaco hide. The front of the tent is generally open, but it can be closed whenever occasion requires. The interior is divided into partitions, each inmate having his own bunk, where he sleeps and where his gear and chattels are stowed away when not in use.

I entered one of these tents, and looked about me. In the front part there were three or four small fires, round each of which sat a circle of Indians, who were warming their toes, and smoking or taking maté. The squaws were all hard at work, sewing capas, weaving fillets, or tying up bundles of ostrich feathers. At my approach they stopped working, and broke into a chorus of guttural commentaries on my appearance, interspersed with a great deal of noisy laughter, which they kept up till I left the tent. Little children and dogs were sprawling about the place in all directions, apparently on very good terms with each other,—a dog not unfrequently gnawing at one end of a piece of meat, off the other end of which a young Tehuelche hopeful was making his dinner. In another corner was a group deeply immersed in the chances and changes of a game of cards. Some of the Indians are inveterate gamblers, and play for very high stakes indeed. It is not an uncommon thing for a "plunger" to risk all his horses and his saddle-gear, knife and bolas to boot, on the chances of a single game.

We visited all the tents, and then went back to enjoy a pipe by our own fireside. We had not been long seated when quite a deputation of pretty young squaws arrived, to interview us. They bashfully sat down at some distance from our fire, and for a time did nothing but giggle and look shy. At last one of them, the prettiest (artful daughters of Eve!), after a great deal of argument and some persuasive pushing, seemed to consent to become the spokeswoman of the party, and taking courage came boldly up to us, and producing a plate from under her capa, with a very engaging smile she held it out to me, repeating the word "Azucar" several times in a pleading, coaxing tone, which it was impossible to resist. I gave her some sugar and biscuit, with which she returned to her companions, seemingly very much pleased. After having sat for a few minutes longer, just for politeness' sake, as it were, they got up and went back to their homes. They must have reported favourably on the results of their expedition, for they had not been gone long when another lot arrived, who also wanted azucar. We had just doled out a small portion to them, when still another crowd came down upon us, composed chiefly of elderly squaws, each with a plate and such a cheerful desire to see it filled with sugar, that it became necessary to restrain our generous instincts, and stow away the sugar-bags in the depths of our tent. Finding us inexorable, the elders soon took their departure, in great good-humour, and seemingly as happy as if they had got all they wanted.

We were favoured with a great many visits during dinner, and at one time we were the centre of a circle of men, women, and children, two rows deep, who were incessant in their demands for biscuit, sugar, or something, but so calmly indifferent under the inevitable refusal with which, in self-defence, we were obliged to meet all their supplications, that it seemed they really did not care whether they got anything given to them or not. Post-prandially I mused whether, after all, they had not the advantage over me. It is true I had "the cakes and ale;" but then, on the other hand, to make matters even, they had the finely balanced temperament, which enabled them to bear the want of those luxuries with the most perfect equanimity.

After dinner, Garcia sat down to play cards with an Indian. I watched him lose successively his bolas, his lasso, his knife, and his saddle, and when I went to bed he was just commencing another game, for which the stakes were a horse a side. I fully expected to wake up the next morning and find that he had lost his whole troop; but he was not so unfortunate, and when they finally left off playing he was only a pair of bolas to the bad.

VII

SANTA CRUZ AND ITS ENVIRONS

THE next morning, having said good-bye to Isidoro, who was stopping some days with the Indians before coming down to Santa Cruz to accompany me to Sandy Point, we started off at a brisk gallop, which, in about three hours, brought us to the broad valley down which the Santa Cruz River rolls its rapid and tortuous course.

The weather was already sensibly colder than at St. Julian. On our road we encountered several snow and hail storms, and were therefore not sorry when we at last arrived in front of Pavon Island, where there is a small house, built many years ago by an Argentine, who lived there for the purpose of trading with the Indians,—a business still carried on by its present inmate, Don Pedro Dufour.

On hearing our shouts, the inmates of the island, *i.e.* Don Pedro and his peon, came over to us in a small boat, in which our effects and persons were safely transported to the island. The horses and dogs had to swim over as best they could, and a very hard and cold job they must have found it, as the current of the river runs with extreme velocity, something over six miles an hour.

The house into which Don Pedro gave us a hearty welcome, was built of adobe and stones, and contained two dwelling-rooms, a kitchen, and a storeroom. There was another smaller house on the island, used as a storeroom for the sugar, biscuit, aguadiente, etc., which Don Pedro barters with the Indians for guanaco capas and ostrich feathers.

In the long grass behind the house, a troop of horses was grazing, together with four or five fine sheep, with which, judging by their splendid condition, the pasturage of Patagonia evidently agreed. A pig was grunting and clamouring greedily for food in a pen hard by; ducks, pigeons, and other poultry were pecking about the yard; a thrush was singing in a cage hung up outside the house, and altogether there was quite a homely, civilized look about the place, which 1 should not have expected to find, considering that it is the only fixed human habitation in that immense desert, which extends for a distance of some seven hundred miles, from Chubut to Sandy Point,—a desert whose area is twice that of Great Britain, and whose only inhabitants are a few ostrich-hunters and Indians.

Pending Isidoro's arrival, I made several excursions in the neighbourhood of the island, amongst others one to the port of Santa Cruz, where in the hollow of a sheltered ravine stands the settlement of M. Rouquand. The houses, of which there are several, built of timber brought from Buenos Ayres for the purpose, I found to be little the worse for wear or weather.

The cañon where these houses stand is still called " Les Misioneros," for it was there that some missionaries resided in 1863, who laboured for a time at the attempted conversion of the Tehuelches to Christianity, without, however, meeting with the success their endeavours deserved.

It is a pity that M. Rouquand's courageous attempt at colonizing that desert place and founding an industry, whose success would have been an incentive to further enterprise, should have been thwarted by Chili's having taken umbrage at his occupying a miserable piece of ground, of no possible value to anybody, without having previously gone through the formality of asking their ratification of the concession granted him by the Argentine Government.

The port of Santa Cruz is formed by the confluence of the river of that name and its tributary, the Rio Chico, which at this point expands into a broad bay, capable of affording shelter to a number of ships, and of easy access from the ocean, there being about fifty feet of water over the bar at high tide.

The river Santa Cruz varies in breadth from four hundred yards to nearly a mile, and runs along a winding valley, which extends in a direct line to the westward. In 1834 an expedition under Admiral Fitzroy, composed of three light boats, manned by eighteen sailors, started up the river, with the object of ascertaining its source; but having ascended a distance of 140 miles from the sea, and 240 by the course of the river, want of provisions obliged him to turn back, especially as, finding no diminution in the volume of its waters, he inferred that its upper course must be along the base of the Andes, from north to south, and that its source must probably be near that of the Rio Negro, in lat. 45° S.

In this conjecture he was at error, for in 1877 Dr. F. Moreno successfully determined the source of the Santa Cruz as being taken from a lake situated in lat. 50° 14′ S., and long. 71° 59′ W. some miles from Lake Viedma, with which, however, it has no visible communication. This fine sheet of water measures thirty miles from east to west, and ten miles at its greatest breadth; its depth Dr. Moreno was unable to ascertain,—with a line of 120 feet he could find no bottom at a short distance from the shore.

According to the same authority the greatest depth of the river is seventy feet, but the rapidity of the current, in some places as much as fifteen miles an hour, must have prevented reliable soundings being taken.

Near Lake Viedma is a volcano, the Chalten, which, according to the Indians, still throws out quantities of ashes. At the time Dr. Moreno was there, a column of smoke was issuing from its crater.

The country around Santa Cruz River differs in no way from that I had already traversed, one of the peculiarities of Patagonian landscape being its complete sameness. The plains, which occupy the greater portion of the country, extend along the Atlantic Ocean. The line separating them from the fertile mountain regions is extremely sharply defined. Beginning at Cape Negro, Magellan Straits, lat. 53°S. and long. 75° 50′ W., it runs thence west-north-west to the north-eastern extremity of Otway Water, following the channels of Fitzroy Passage, and the northern shores of Skyring Water to long. 72° W., and then extends along the eastern shores of Obstruction Sound and Kirke Water, running then due northward towards Lake Viedma. These plains rise almost uniformly, 300 feet high, one above another, like terraces, and are traversed occasionally by ravines and flat-bottomed depressions, which latter frequently contain salt lakes. The formation of the country is tertiary, resting on porphyry and quartz, ridges of which often protrude through the surface. Near long. 70° W. the plains are capped with a layer of lava, about a hundred miles in width.

Darwin accounts for the regularity with which the plains rise one over the other by the supposition that the land has been raised in a mass from under the sea, the upheaving movement having been interrupted by at least eight long periods of rest, during which the sea ate deeply back into the land, forming at successive levels the long lines of escarpments which separate the different plains.

In that strange country the vegetable kingdom is as little varied as the aspect of the landscape: from Chubut to Sandy Point, from the sea-coast to the Cordilleras, one meets the same few species of miserable stunted bushes and coarse grasses.

The following is a cut showing the formation of the country at Port St. Julian[1]:—

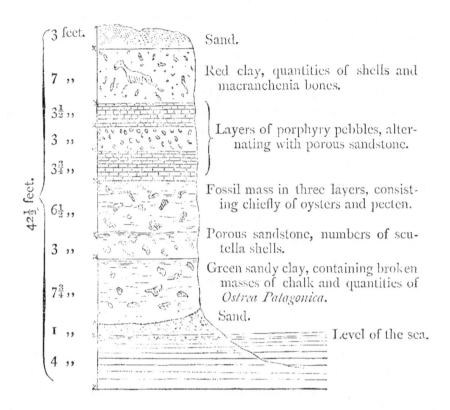

Of bushes, the most frequent are the jume (*Salecemia*) and the calafaté (*Berberis axifolia*). The former plant is remarkably rich in soda, as will be seen by the following analysis of its ash :—

Chloride of sodium	19˙38
Sulphate of lime	9˙50
Carbonate of magnesia	1˙94
Phosphate of potash	12˙15
Carbonate of potash	7˙50
Silicate of soda	7˙80
Carbonate of soda	41˙73
	——————
	100˙00

Though they are so little favoured by nature, still I must confess that in the sober-hued Patagonian landscapes, with their grave breadth and stern severity of outline, and in the grand monotony of solemn silence and solitude pervading their barren plains, there is something which has left a far deeper impression on my mind than has the brightest and most varied tropical scenery. Standing in the midst of one of those seemingly endless plains, one experiences an indefinable feeling of awe, akin to that which the contemplation of the ocean produces, only, perhaps, more impressively grand; for the ocean is ever noisy and restless, the pampa eternally silent and still.

During my stay at Santa Cruz, nothing of importance occurred, if I may except a ball given by the Indians at the Rio Chico, in honour of somebody's marriage or funeral, I forget which. An Indian who came to the island to get the rum, which is a *sine quâ non* at all their entertainments, invited us to assist at the ball,—an offer which we readily accepted.

On arriving at the camp a very lively scene presented itself to our eyes. As is customary on such occasions, several mares had been killed, and roasting and boiling was going on at numerous fires. Every one was feasting in the greatest good-humour, which on our approach was further heightened, scouts having already brought the news that we were coming with the aguadiente.

The advent of the latter was greeted with loud acclamations; some of the older men gathered round the cask, which was speedily tapped, and then with great unction and solemnity they proceeded to taste the liquor, in order to see whether it had been over-watered. Several decided grunts of satisfaction, however, showed that these aged fathers approved of its strength; whereupon a general and doubtless equitable distribution of the spirit took place, and before long the whole camp, men, women, and children, had ample opportunities for judging of its merits for themselves.

Presently a dance was organized. The men who took part in it were all specially painted for the occasion, and wore long feathers on their heads. The dance itself was a monotonous jig, executed to the excruciating music of various drums or tom-toms. The women, strange to say, do not dance; at least, they did not as long as they were sober.

As the evening wore on, after vast quantities of meat had been consumed and innumerable dances had been performed, special attention began to be paid to the aguadiente, and the fun consequently soon began to get very fast and very furious.

Long before midnight every one was more or less drunk, and the ball which had commenced with becoming order and solemnity had now degenerated into a wild orgy. The flames from the different fires, strangely blended with the pale moonlight, cast a lurid glare on the dusky bodies and painted faces of the revellers, who, mad with excitement and drink, were dancing, singing, and whooping, in deafening concert. A more gruesome scene it were hard to imagine. It seemed as if the imps of darkness were celebrating their unearthly rites in this desert spot, and I half expected, at any moment, to see the whole crew vanish, with a flash and a bang, into the bowels of the earth, leaving the orthodox smell of sulphur behind them.

Nothing of the sort occurred, however, though I presently received a shock almost as startling as any supernatural event could have been. An old squaw, who was painfully of this world and the vanities thereof, and who had previously been addressing me for some time in the most eloquent of gutturals, finding that nothing could melt my icy demeanour, as a last resource suddenly threw her arms round my unsuspecting neck, and hugged me in a greasy embrace.

With great difficulty I managed to free myself, whereupon I ran away towards some other part of the camp, to escape further annoyance. Had this old beldame been acquainted with woman's privileges on such occasions, she would have known that, under the circumstances, the correct thing to have done was to have fainted or become hysterical. But nothing could have been further from the thoughts of this unenlightened savage,—the impulse of her untrained mind being to run after me as hard as her legs could carry her. And the rest of the Indians, with one of those sudden whims drunken people are liable to, took it into their heads to join in the chase, and I soon had the whole crowd shrieking and howling at my heels. What their intentions were I don't know, nor did I feel inclined to discover; fortunately, before they came up to me I reached my horse, which I had left ready saddled, and galloping swiftly away, I soon left them behind me.

I was presently joined by Garcia and the others, who had taken the same opportunity to escape in order to avoid the rows with which these balls frequently wind up. They are not often attended by actual bloodshed, however, as the squaws, with naïve foresight, generally hide all weapons before the ceremonies commence. We reached Santa Cruz shortly after daybreak, and so ended my first experience of a Tehuelche merry-making.

I called at the camp the next day, to pay my *visite de digestion*, and made a point of going to the tent where the old squaw, who was so near becoming *teterrima causa belli*, abode. She had a bad headache, and looked very demure and penitent. I rallied her with smiles, and attempted, by my assiduous attentions, to make up for my discourteous behaviour of the previous evening. But she took no notice of me, and received all my overtures with the utmost indifference It was a case of—

"The devil was sick; the devil a saint would be."

1. From a perforation made by E. de Ville Massot, C.E.

VIII

A TROUBLING DELAY

SHORTLY after, on the 2nd of October, Isidoro came over to Pavon Island, with his horses and some 250 lbs. of ostrich feathers sewn up in hides, which he was going to take down to Sandy Point to barter, and I accordingly made the necessary arrangements for accompanying him.

Never was a more unlucky trip commenced under more unfavourable auspices.

I was extremely unwell, and my indisposition increased with every hour. Isidoro, in crossing over to the island, had lost his whip in the river, and he seemed to consider this a sure omen of misfortune. The mishap threw quite a gloom over his mind, and he almost decided on giving up the journey altogether. With great difficulty I persuaded him to relinquish this intention, though I little thought, as I did so, that I was indirectly drawing him to his ruin.

The weather, too, was unpropitious. Twice heavy showers of rain made us turn back when on the point of starting. We had already unsaddled our horses and put off our departure till the next day; but towards midday the sun again shone out, and that finally decided us to make a definite start.

As we calculated that our journey to Sandy Point would last about eight days, we took but few provisions; and in order to spare the pack-horse as much as possible, we left our tent behind, trusting to the weather not to be too severe upon us. The cavalcade consisted of Isidoro, Guillaume, and myself, twenty-eight horses, and five dogs.

Having said good-bye to Don Pedro, Garcia, and Maximo, who were remaining at Santa Cruz, we mounted our horses, forded the river, and got under route.

We had not gone far when the weather again changed for the worse. A drizzling sleet—half rain, half snow—began to fall, and a thick mist settled down on the hills, giving an indescribably mournful appearance to the at all times gloomy country.

We rode along in the lowest of spirits and in the midst of a cheerless silence, broken only by the patter of the rain or the splashing of our horses hoofs over the marshy ground. As we went on my headache grew more and more violent, and every movement of the horse made me wince with pain; but not wishing to turn back now that we were once off, I bore up as well as I could for several hours, till at last, burning with fever and thoroughly exhausted with the efforts I had made to subdue my sufferings, I fairly began to reel in my saddle, and, finding it impossible to continue any longer on horseback, I called out to my companions to halt.

Although we were just in the middle of a bare plain, there was fortunately a little grass growing round the borders of a small sheet of water near where I dismounted, or otherwise, on account of the horses, we should have been obliged to continue till we got to the next ravine, which was still a considerable distance off.

They made a bed for me under a low bush, and I was glad to be able to lie down. I suffered intensely all through the night, tossing sleeplessly about, and longing for dawn to appear.

The morning found me in such a state that, much to my own and my companions' regret, it was quite impossible to continue the journey, though, had I foreseen the consequences of that one day's delay, I would have gone on, even if I had had to be lashed to the saddle.

It was altogether a very miserable time. It is pleasant enough to roam over the pampa when you are strong and well, and can enjoy a good gallop after an ostrich in that pure, inspiriting air, when the coarsest food seems delicious, and you can sleep as soundly on the hardest couch as on the softest feather bed; but it is another thing when you are sick and in pain, and miss the darkened room, the tempting viands, the cooling drinks, and the thousand devices which make sickness less trying. When, instead, you have to face the weary pangs of illness, exposed alternately to the glaring sun shine and the cold rain showers, stretched on the bare ground, a hard saddle for your pillow, a miserable bush your sole shelter against the cutting wind, then, like me, you will probably lose a little of your enthusiasm for the romantic life of the pampa, and sigh for the comforts of humdrum civilization.

The next day my anxiety to reach Sandy Point as early as possible, urged me to declare that I felt well enough to continue the journey, and enabled me to support the unintermitting pains the movement of the horse inflicted on my sore body, which, without the assistance of so strong a motive, I should hardly have been able to do.

However, I gradually got better, and by the time we reached Coy Inlet, which was on the fourth day after leaving Santa Cruz, I felt all right again. We found Coy Inlet River rather swollen, but the ford was still quite passable, from which circumstance we concluded that that of the river Gallegos would be equally so,—a matter of congratulation for us, as at that time of the year the snows melt in the Cordilleras, and the rivers are frequently impassable for several days together.

We were in high spirits over that evening's supper, and already began calculating how many nights we had yet to pass before we should be able to go to sleep, heedless of wind or rain, under roof in Sandy Point. It was the last cheerful evening we were to pass for a long time to come, though we little dreamt it.

The following morning we started for our next stage, Rio Gallegos, which is about fifty miles from Coy Inlet.

The pace we travelled at was a kind of amble, half trot, half canter, though occasionally, when the nature of the ground we were riding over permitted, we would break into an easy gallop. The horses of Patagonia are remarkable for their endurance; seventy or eighty miles a day over that most trying country, with its rapid succession of steep escarpments, seems nothing to them, and if at the end of the day's journey an ostrich starts up, they will answer to the spur and dash away after it as fresh and as gamely as if they had just been saddled.

The guanacos seemed more numerous than ever in the plains we were now crossing; some herds which swept past us, I think, must have numbered quite six or seven hundred head. They gave us far more trouble than we gave them, for every now and then the dogs, who with difficulty could keep cool in the presence of such abundance of game, would make a dash at some peculiarly tempting quarry, only to be brought back to their masters' heels, after much whistling and shouting, thereby causing considerable delay in our onward progress.

On this day I was particularly struck with the change in the temperature, which had been gradually growing colder since we left Santa Cruz, and which was now already unpleasantly raw and severe. Over the plain, too, there was a keen wind blowing, which seemed to go right through one, and we were glad when we at last reached a long ravine called the Ravine of the Squaws, which leads down from the plains into Gallegos valley. It bears this name because, when coming from Coy Inlet, the Indian women always enter the valley by that route. As they then form in single file, the hoofs of so many horses following in each other's wake have gradually worn several deep but narrow trails into the soil. The men ride down anywhere, without reference to the movements of the squaws, who always approach their camps from exactly the same points. The Indians change their camps with tolerable regularity according to the time of the year. They generally pass the winter together in Coy Inlet or Gallegos valley, and in spring, after the young guanaco hunting is over, they break up and disperse; some going to the Cordilleras, others to Santa Cruz, and others again to Sandy Point, though the latter settlement is never honoured with their presence long, as there is not sufficient pasturage for the horses in that region, and the dogs, too, have to subsist on very short rations, as ostriches are rather scarce in the vicinity of Sandy Point, and guanacos do not range so far south.

Presently a turn of the ravine brought us in full view of the valley, though the river itself was as yet invisible. A few minutes would now settle all doubts as to the state of the ford. We broke into a gallop, craning our necks anxiously to get a glimpse of the water, in rather dubious suspense. It was of material importance for me to take the steamer of the 15th of that month, and if the river was unfordable I knew we might have to wait for at least eight days before the waters would subside, and that delay would cause me to lose my steamer.

Suddenly Isidoro, who was some way ahead, drew in his reins and stopped short, turning round with a look of blank dismay on his brown face, which told but too plainly that our worst fears were realized. With drooping reins we rode slowly on till we got to the river, now no longer the shallow stream which in summer one can wade over knee-deep, but a broad torrent, which eddied, swirled, and foamed, as it dashed rapidly over its stormy bed through banks which were already growing too narrow for its swollen waters. In the middle we could still see a single tuft of long grass, which was bending with the current, and this, Isidoro told me, grew on a little island, which when the river is fordable, is several feet above the water's level. Twenty-four hours ago it had doubtless been high and dry. We had arrived just a day too late,—the day lost on account of my illness!

We stood for some time in silence, staring blankly at the obstacle which had suddenly sprung up to bar our progress, with a feeling of utter disgust and helplessness; and then, the first shock of the disappointment over, we began to discuss the chances in favour of a speedy fall of the water. Isidoro was of opinion, from previous acquaintance with the river at that season, that in eight days at the most, it would have sunk to its ordinary level, two or three consecutive days of frost being quite sufficient to arrest the thawing of the snows on the Cordilleras, and to cause the river to fall as rapidly as it had risen.

But even eight days seemed a long time to look forward to; eight days to be passed in tiresome inaction and constant exposure to the weather, and we now bitterly regretted not having brought the tent with us. Our provisions, too, had only been calculated for a ten days' trip, and were already almost exhausted. Though, of course, we need never want for meat, still lean meat, without salt or any farinaceous adjunct, is not the kind of diet to keep up one's strength in cold weather, and under all sorts of exertions and hardships. All these disagreeables, however, seemed slight ones, compared with the misfortune of having lost the steamer of the 15th, by which, for pressing reasons, I ought to have immediately proceeded to Buenos Ayres. There was now no other chance of leaving Sandy Point till the 30th. Isidoro, too, had some reason to be concerned at the delay, for if he did not reach the settlement soon, he knew the price of feathers would have fallen considerably, and he would make but a bad bargain. Altogether, it was with heavy hearts that we slowly turned from the river, in search of some suitable spot for camping at. In that respect we were unfortunate also, not being able to find a sheltering bush anywhere. Gallegos is the favourite camping-place of the Indians during several months of the year, and consequently any bushes which may formerly have existed in the immediate neighbourhood of the valley, had long been broken up by the squaws for firewood. Finally, we had to camp on the open, about three miles from the river, sheltered slightly on one side by the tall escarpment which bounds one side of the valley, but exposed on all others to whatever wind might choose to blow, and if it should happen to rain we had of course no means of keeping anything dry.

Another inconvenience of not having some bush to camp under was that the fire was completely at the mercy of the wind, and flared away without emitting any warmth, blinding those who sat round it with smoke, and making it very difficult to cook anything properly. With the packages containing Isidoro's feathers we managed to rig up a kind of makeshift to obviate this difficulty, and then we all three set about looking for firewood, to collect which we had to wander about for a long time, as the whole country round seemed to have been swept bare of that necessary by the Indians.

We were not very cheerful over our dinner that evening, as may be imagined. The fire burned badly, the air was cold and damp, and soon after our meal we rolled ourselves in our furs, and prepared to pass the first of the many nights we were fated to sleep through on the banks of the river Gallegos.

IX

ON THE BANKS OF THE GALLEGOS

MY first thought on waking the next morning was, of course, the river. During the night, in a moment of wakefulness, a steady rumbling noise, the rush of distant water, had struck on my listening ear, and I was accordingly prepared to find a further rise in the river at daylight. But the sight which now met my gaze took me by surprise, notwithstanding. The whole of the lower-lying portion of the valley, as far as the eye could reach, was one sheet of water, and the flood was almost visibly rising towards those parts which yet remained dry. The river itself was no longer distinguishable, being confounded with the general mass of water, but we could plainly hear the dull roar of its mighty current, which was still sweeping down with unabated force, bearing on its curling waters huge trunks of trees, which, perhaps, but the day before, had been torn from the distant Cordilleras.

On account of the high position of our camp, we were, as yet, far from the flood, though, if it continued to rise as rapidly as hitherto, we might soon have to move further on.

Isidoro, too, was quite aghast at the dimensions the inundation was assuming. He had never seen the river so swollen before, and began seriously to doubt whether, in a fortnight even, we should be able to cross over, as there was no knowing how long the rise would continue. The snowfall of the past winter had been heavier than any of the oldest Indians could remember, and it might reasonably be supposed that the spring floods would be proportionately unusual in volume and duration.

We passed all that day in gloomy forebodings, watching the progress of the water. At night-time it was still steadily rising. The following morning we found the flood had risen to within fifteen feet of our camp; but we had the satisfaction of finding that it was already abating, for during the night it had been several feet higher, as evinced by the marks left on the grass. Indeed, all day it kept on falling, and so rapidly that we commenced to speculate on whether the river might not eventually subside as quickly as it had risen, and allow us to cross over, after all, within the eight days we had from the first considered as the probable duration of our enforced stay at Gallegos.

The next day again brought despondency. The water seemed to have remained stationary during the night, and there was a change for the worse in the weather. The thick mist which had accompanied daybreak resolved itself, as the morning wore on, into a steady, heavy rainfall, which seemed grimly resolved to reduce us to the last stage of misery and discomfort.

We covered up our furs with the packages of feathers, so as, if possible, to have something dry for bedtime; and then cowered round the drooping fire in resigned helplessness, whilst it rained and rained down upon us with merciless pertinacity.

There is nothing so trying as having to sit hour after hour in dejected silence, exposed to a cold rain-storm, which you know may possibly last for days, and from which you have absolutely no shelter, feeling, as time goes on, the damp gradually creeping through your clothes, till it at last reaches the skin and chills you to the bone, while occasional rills of water run off your back hair and trickle icily down your shivering neck, till you are thoroughly drenched and numbed and cramped with cold.

We passively sat shivering in this wretched plight till long after noon, getting up now and then to have a look at the weather or to stretch our stiffened limbs. At last the clouds began to break up, the storm collected its dying force in one last fierce downpour, and then ceased altogether, giving us just time to dry our clothes and bodies with the aid of a good fire, before night came on.

The days dragged their slow length along, and at last a week, which, in the weariness of eternally watching and waiting, seemed more like a month, had gone past without any signs of a speedy abatement in the height of the river. The waters had fallen, it is true, and were still falling, but how slowly and sluggishly!

Day after day I used to climb up the tall escarpment bounding the northern plain, from the top of which a good view was to be obtained of the valley, which was now one vast sheet of water, dotted here and there with green islands, a long line of foam showing where the course of the river lay. There I would sit for hours, watching how little tufts of grass would gradually enlarge into islands, which in their turn would slowly grow and grow till they joined and formed part of the mainland, which was slowly but steadily reclaiming its lost domains from the retreating waters. This was my only occupation; I had no heart to join Isidoro on his frequent hunting expeditions; the river was my sole thought, the only topic of conversation in which I could take any interest, and beside that everything else was of the utmost indifference.

It was not that I had any actual fear of losing the steamer of the 30th, especially after the eighth day of our sojourn, during which the water had fallen with such surprising quickness that the banks of the river were in some parts beginning to uncover again. Still, occasionally, the fact that it was just within the limits of possibility that I might not be able to pass in time would obtrude itself unpleasantly on my mind; and though I would immediately triumphantly argue any such idea away, yet I felt that nothing was absolutely sure till we were actually on the other side of the river, and, pending that event, I was in a continual state of worry and restlessness.

When we had been nine days at Guaraiké, as that part of Gallegos is called by the Indians, Isidoro suggested, in view of the late rapid fall of the water, that we should go to another pass, some forty miles further up the river, which he thought might perhaps be fordable before the one we were now at.

Any change was welcome to me; I had got to know and grow weary of every line, every curve of the country, every stone almost, round our present camp, and leaving them seemed a step towards crossing the river. It was, therefore, with a comparatively light heart that I helped to drive up, pack, and saddle the horses, and soon we were off for the "Paso del Medio," or Middle Pass, as it is called.

As usual there was a boisterous wind blowing upon the plains, though far colder and sharper than any we had as yet experienced. In fact, the weather, instead of daily growing warmer, had been steadily becoming colder and colder, and of late snow-squalls had become of quite frequent occurrence.

Several hours' riding brought us to the Middle Pass. Before camping we rode down to inspect the state of the water. At Guaraiké we had been unable to approach the river itself, as all the land on our side had been flooded over; but here at one spot the river bent in towards the northern side of the valley, and flowed for some distance along a steep cliff, which, of course, it could not overflow, and we were thus enabled to go down to its very brink, which was in so far satisfactory as it enabled us to gauge with more exactness the rise or fall of the flood.

I drove a stake into the bank, and notched it at the water's level, and then we went back to a bush we had selected for camping under. It was rather a small one, and, being upon the plain, was exposed to the full force of the wind. However, it was the most suitable place we could find, and with the aid of some drift-wood, quantities of which were lying along the banks of the river, we managed to build up a kind of one-walled hut, which formed a tolerable shelter against the wind. The latter, during the whole of my stay in Patagonia, blew almost uninterruptedly from the west, either more or less cold, according as it came from the north-west or south-west.

That evening we ate our last biscuit; our other provisions had already been exhausted, and hence-forward we were reduced to a regimen of guanaco and ostrich meat, *pur et simple*, without salt even, for our small stock of that necessary, notwithstanding careful nursing, had also gradually thinned away.

At first the results of this exclusively meat diet were very unpleasant. However much I would eat at a meal—and the quantity of meat I consumed at times was incredible—half an hour afterwards I would feel as famished as if I had touched nothing for days; in fact, I seemed to derive no nourishment at all from my food. As time went on, however, I got more used to the change, and soon ceased to experience so phenomenal and troublesome an appetite, though, of course, I grew very weak, and had it not been for the ostriches' eggs we occasionally found, and which kept up my stamina a little, I should not have had sufficient strength to support me through the exertions I was subsequently called upon to make.

It became quite an important event when, as now and then happened, we managed to kill a puma, as we were then enabled to indulge in fat meat. On these occasions, I remember, I used to feel rather disgusted at the voracity with which we all used to gorge ourselves on the fat, without biscuit, salt, or any other condiment. But when one passes days and days, eating nothing but the leanest and most tasteless of meat, and more especially in cold weather, one feels a hankering for fat, as strong as the habitual drunkard's craving for alcohol.

The day after our arrival at the Paso del Medio, the waters commenced to retire at a rapid pace, and such improvement shortly took place in the state of things, that we quite looked forward to being able to cross in three or four days.

The water had disappeared everywhere except in close vicinity to the river, which still looked of formidable breadth, however, though its banks were for the most part uncovered. We had had several sharp frosts, and the weather had continued bitterly cold, to which fortunate circumstance we attributed the corresponding speedy abatement in the water. But now came two successive days of warm sunshine, and, though the water still continued to fall, Isidoro grew apprehensive of a fresh thaw taking place in the Cordilleras, before the effects of the first flood had subsided sufficiently to allow of our passing the river.

This new danger threatening us gave me extreme uneasiness. I had already observed how sensitive the river was to the state of the temperature, its fall varying in measure as the weather, in the preceding one or two days, had been more or less cold, and I therefore looked doubtfully forward to the morrow for the effects of the before-mentioned comparatively warm days.

Our apprehensions were unfortunately but too well founded. The next day I had no need to go down to examine the notch on the stake, to find out whether the river had fallen or risen. Without leaving our camp, which was at some distance from the valley, one could see but too plainly that a fresh flood had taken place during the night. The banks of the river had disappeared; and half the valley was under water again. Thus one night had undone all the progress of several days, and our chances of crossing the river had become as problematical as they had been ten days ago.

This was a heavy, disheartening blow to me. Now it was indeed difficult to foresee when we might be able to pass. Any attempt at calculating the event was gratuitous in the face of what had just happened. The water might rise and fall in the same manner a dozen times. The unusual fall of snow that winter might entail, and had in fact already entailed, unusual consequences. We might be kept waiting for weeks, and months even, during which my friends would be kept in a state of great anxiety and suspense as to my fate; and, apart from these considerations, now that the charm of novelty had worn off, the life of hardship and isolation I was leading had become extremely distasteful to me; a deep *ennui* fell upon me, which I could not shake off, and which the society of my companions was not calculated to dissipate. I impatiently longed for those refinements and associations of civilization, from which, at the outset of my trip, I had thought it pleasant to escape.

Under the influence of all these feelings, I resolved to attempt to swim the river. On the first day of our arrival at Guaraiké I had seriously entertained this plan, but I had then rejected it as being attended with considerable danger, and also because I had hoped that in a few days the river might be fordable. The danger was now, of course, still greater; but the prospect of an indefinite prolongation of my present unbearable position was so terrible that I felt ready for any enterprise, however risky, which might free me from it.

Guillaume, to whom I communicated my intentions, thought my idea was practicable, and declared himself ready to accompany me whenever I chose. He, too, was anxious to get to Sandy Point for several reasons, of which the chief one was that he had no tobacco left, and life without it, he seemed to think, was not worth living.

It was now the 18th October, and if we crossed the river by the 26th we had plenty of time to get to Sandy Point by the 1st November, on or about which day the next steamer passed for Buenos Ayres. We therefore deferred the carrying out of our plans for a few days, in order to await a fresh fall in the water.

I felt much more tranquil now that I had made up my mind to take the bull by the horns, and my companions were surprised at the sudden change of my spirits, which henceforward were more cheerful and buoyant than they had been for a long time.

X

ATTEMPTS TO CROSS THE RIVER

WE stopped two days longer at the Paso del Medio, and then, tormented with continual restlessness, we moved thirty miles further up, to the last pass, called the "Paso de Alquinta."

We camped at about six miles from the pass itself, under shelter of what Isidoro, rather grandiloquently, persisted in calling a "house," but which was in reality nothing but three low walls, barely four feet high, built by some Indian traders, of blocks of lava, the chinks between which were stopped with mud and grass.

The "house" was, of course, roofless, and by no means so good a lodging as a thick bush would have been, but still it was better than nothing, and at all events enabled us to have always a good fire burning, without consuming too much fuel,—a very important consideration, as there was very little wood to be met with anywhere in that region.

During the first night there was a heavy fall of snow, and on waking I felt an unusual weight on my furs, and under them an excessive warmth I was certainly not accustomed to. Thrusting out my head, I found everything covered with snow. The distant hills stood out in glittering relief against the dark grey sky, and the whole landscape was specklessly white, except where the river flowed along the valley, looking inky black by contrast with the surrounding country. Our horses, poor animals, plentifully besprinkled with snow, too, were standing near to the camp, herded motionless together, with sadly drooping heads, and an expression of patient suffering and forlorn misery in their rough faces, which filled me with compassion for them.

We remained in bed till the afternoon, when the snow began to thaw away, soaking all our bedding and making things generally uncomfortable for us.

Fearing the effect the melting of the recent snow might have on the river, we resolved to make an attempt to cross it the following morning. Isidoro, to whom we now communicated our intention for the first time, seemed quite alarmed at the idea, and did everything in his power to persuade us to desist from it. Until this occasion, I had never been able to get more than half a dozen words out of him at a time; but now, in his efforts to induce us to give up our undertaking, which he qualified as an act of utter madness, he waxed quite eloquent, and made a longer speech than he had probably ever delivered himself of in his whole existence. The current, he urged, was too strong for our horses to stem; moreover, a companion of his, he told us, had once tried to cross the river when it was not nearly so swollen as now, and had narrowly escaped being drowned. Finding, however, that we had made up our minds, and were not to be persuaded to alter them, Isidoro relapsed into his usual silence, whilst we made our preparations for the ensuing day.

We intended crossing over at sunrise, so as to have ample time to dry our wet things on the other side before night-time. In order to be able to rely on having something dry to cover ourselves with immediately after our swim over, we rolled two capas up as tightly as possible, and stuffed them into a small water-tight canvas bag. In the middle of the capas we carefully placed our greatest treasure—twelve wax matches in a little tortoise-shell box, which we rendered impervious to damp by securely wrapping it in pieces of guanaco hide.

Of matches, I must mention, we had run short, as of everything else, and were compelled to be most economical in the use of the few that still remained to us, to which end the fire was kept burning day and night. We put into our saddle bags sufficient ostrich meat and puma fat to last us for three days,—the time we calculated we should require to reach Sandy Point in. Guillaume intended leaving his dogs with Isidoro, as they would suffer unnecessarily from the fatigue of such a rapid journey.

Having concluded our preparations, we sat down to dinner, over which we discussed our chances for the morrow, and arranged our plan of action. There were two ways of crossing over—either we might swim over on horseback, or put our clothes and things on the horses and make them swim over first, and then follow ourselves as soon as they had safely arrived on the opposite shore.

The objection to the first method was that the horses' strength might possibly give way in the middle of the river, or that by some accident we might be unseated at a distance from the shore, in either of which cases, encumbered with our clothes, etc., we were almost certain to be drowned. The difficulty which presented itself in connection with the second method was the doubt we felt as to whether we should be able to stand a long immersion in the icy cold water without succumbing to cramp and exhaustion, especially taking into consideration the weak state our late poor diet had reduced us to. After a long discussion, we finally adopted the plan of swimming over on horseback.

We went to bed early, but it was a long time before I could fall asleep; I was too excited with the thoughts of the coming struggle. At last I was to try conclusions with the river, which had so long baffled me. If successful, four nights from then I should be at Sandy Point, sure of my steamer, relieved from the hardships I was now suffering, and soon to be restored to civilization, for which I was longing as ardently as an Indian, confined to the close, noisy streets of a populous town, might long for the breezy solitudes of the pampa. In my dreams that night I must have crossed the river twenty times at least, and I

was splashing in the midst of its cold current for the twenty-first time, when Guillaume woke me up, to tell me it was time to get ready.

Day was just breaking, and the weather was cloudy and cold. We ate a hurried breakfast, saddled our horses, and rode down towards the pass, which was about six miles from where we were camping. On the way we had to cross the open, and came full under the blast of the bitter wind, which was especially sharp at that early hour; and we were blue and shivering long before we got to the river. There was unfortunately no sun, though I would have given anything for a sight of his cheering face to keep up my *morale*, which, I must confess, at the prospect of a cold and dangerous plunge on that wintry morning, had sunk extremely low. Presently we reached the river and never, I thought, had it seemed so broad or looked so unpleasantly dark and treacherous as now. Its eddying current slid past us with a rapidity which made me giddy to watch long. The water foamed viciously as it broke into waves, and showers of spray, swept up by occasional gusts of wind, flew over its troubled surface.

Without further delay, we said good-bye to Isidoro, tightened our saddle-girths, and rode towards the point from which we intended starting. There we paused a moment before taking the decisive step forward,—a moment, of extreme nervous tension for both of us. I felt an oppressive contraction of the throat and chest, which, to be candid, I must attribute to a passing feeling of fear that came over me at the last moment, now that I was about to commit myself, not without serious misgivings as to the consequences, to the mercies of the broad torrent which had so long baffled my progress. However, remembering that the longer one looks at a leap the less one likes to take it, I called out to Guillaume that I was ready, and, with spur and whip, we urged our horses down the steep bank towards the water.

For a moment, rearing and snorting, they instinctively recoiled from the dangerous element, but the pebbly bank giving way under their feet, they could not stop themselves, and down we went—plunge!—head over ears into the cold water. I came to the surface, snapping for breath, but still in the saddle, though the water, dripping over my eyes, for a second or two quite blinded me.

After a little urging, the horses at first struck out right enough, but I found that to keep my seat the greatest exertions were required. Till then I had never swum on horseback, and had no idea how difficult it is to remain in the saddle during the process. The water insinuates itself cunningly between your knees and thighs, imperceptibly you lose your grip, and before you know it, you are gently lifted from your seat, and find yourself afloat, especially when dealing with a current as strong as the one in question.

In the mean time our horses went all right till they came to the middle current, which swept down with great force. The moment they felt it, they suddenly swerved, and made for the bank we had just left. I tried to make my horse turn again, but it became quite unmanageable, and Guillaume in similar attempt was unseated, and was only able to regain his saddle after a severe struggle, which I watched with intense anxiety, as I was unable to go to his rescue, being myself in difficulties.

Breathless and dripping, and humiliated with the consciousness of our failure, we finally got to shore again, and after a hasty council, resolved to make another attempt the following day, as, after the facer we had just received, our nerves were not equal to another ordeal for the present. As long as the excitement of the danger lasted, we had felt neither wet nor cold, but now that it was over Nature reasserted herself, and, drenched to the skin as we were, and exposed to the blasts of a savagely inclement wind, we were completely prostrated, quaking, and shivering, and in such a state that it would have been mere foolhardiness to go into the water again. The six-miles' ride back to the camp in our wet clothes was another disagreeable trial. By the time we got there we were perfectly numbed, and had to warm our stiffened fingers a long time by the fire before they were sufficiently supple to enable us to undress. Having stripped, I rolled myself in my capa, and, thanks to that never-sufficiently-to- be-praised covering, warmth and circulation were soon restored to my chilled limbs. We had, unfortunately, no maté left, though on this occasion we stood more than ever in need of its stimulating and restorative aid.

Notwithstanding our failure, we were by no means disheartened, or disposed to relinquish our endeavours to cross the river; on the contrary, the non-success of our first attempt only intensified my firm resolve to reach Sandy Point, come what might, by the 1st of November, and nerved us to a fresh encounter with the dangers of the river and the inclemency of the weather.

The next morning we again made the attempt, and were again unsuccessful as before. The horses went well till they got to the rapid middle current, and there nothing would induce them to continue. In the struggle with my horse I was swept from my seat. I caught successively at the mane and saddle, but missed them both, just managing to catch hold of a valise which was strapped to the back of the latter. I clung to it like grim death, whilst my horse swam back to the bank. Several times I was in danger of being dragged under by the current, and the valise, under the strain of my weight, began gradually to give way. When it did come down, saddle and all, we were fortunately already in shallow water, and I came to no harm, though it was lucky it held so long, for, heavily booted and clothed as I was, had it happened a little sooner I should have gone to the bottom.

We rode disconsolately back to the camp, suffering extremely from the cold wind, as on the previous day. It was useless, we had now convinced ourselves, to swim over on our horses, for as soon as we came to the middle current we were at their mercy. We therefore resolved to try the other expedient, of driving them over first, and then following ourselves.

For topographical reasons we considered the pass at Guaraiké to be more favourable for this mode of crossing than the one we were now at, and we therefore resolved to go there. We said good-bye once more to Isidoro, who preferred remaining where he was, as there was better pasturage for his horses. We took enough meat with us to last us four days, and leaving the dogs with Isidoro, we started off for Guaraiké, where we arrived late in the evening, after a long gallop.

We did not camp on the old spot, but rode further down to a little "house" Guillaume knew of, similar to the one at the Paso de Alquinta, but with rather higher walls, and which had also been built by some Indian traders.

We ate a very small supper, as it was necessary to economize the little meat we had with us, consoling ourselves with the hope of soon being able to indulge in less meagre fare, and finally we went to bed, confident of passing the next night on the other side of the Gallegos.

XI

HUNGER AND MISFORTUNE

EARLY the next morning, we were up and off to the river. To get to its banks, we had to ride through about a mile and a half of slack water, of varying depth, but seldom above the knees of our horses. Near the river there was a dry spot on a tract of high-lying land, and there accordingly we made our preparations. We took off our clothes, and placed them, together with the matches, revolvers, etc., in the middle of the capas, which were rolled up in the canvas bag, as on the previous occasions, and then carefully and firmly strapped on the saddle of one of the horses. All this was done as quickly as possible, for we were now, of course, almost naked, and the wind, as usual, was blowing hard and cold, with mingled hail and snow. We had little doubt as to the success of this our third effort. Indeed, we had, as it were, cut off our own retreat, in putting all our clothes and furs on the horses, for if they once got safely to the other side, we were of a necessity forced to follow somehow, or expose ourselves to the alternative of perishing with hunger and cold. It was a foolhardy action, but we had become desperate, and were ready to run a slight risk, if only we could surmount the hated obstacle which barred our way to Sandy Point.

Everything being ready, we drove the horses, not without great difficulty, into the water, following ourselves as far as we were able, though such was the force of the current that we had hardly waded in knee-deep before we were knocked off our feet. After immense trouble, with the help of stones and sticks, we managed to drive the horses into the middle current, down whose centre they were soon swept, puffing and snorting and endeavouring to turn back towards the bank we were standing on. Whenever they did so, however, we would fling a volley of stones at them, and by these means at last we got them to head towards the other bank. We watched their progress with beating hearts, in painful suspense lest any accident should happen to them, for they carried, as it were, our own lives, as well as their own. After a few seconds, which seemed an eternity to us, they reached the land, and we gave a shout of joy and relief. But our triumph was of but a second's duration; fate was still against us. As ill luck would have it, the horses happened just to touch land with their noses at a part where the bank was almost vertical, and where they consequently had no footing. Instinctively they turned round and made straight for our side again.

Dismayed and disappointed, we no longer made any attempt to drive them back; indeed, we were fearful that, after their long swim and their efforts against the current, they would not have strength to get back again. At last they landed, however, though of course a long way down from where they had started. We ourselves by this time were in a most pitiable state; for more than half an hour we had been splashing in and out of the icy-cold water, exposed to wind and weather, and we were now thoroughly exhausted, our teeth chattering, our bodies doubled up, and unable to speak to one another except by signs.

We had just strength enough to get the capas out of the bag, the inner ones being fortunately quite dry; and wrapping ourselves well up, we lay down for about an hour, by which time we were sufficiently recovered to be able to remount our horses and ride back to the camp.

We were now at last discouraged. An unexpected stroke of bad luck, a mishap we could not possibly have foreseen, had occurred just at the last moment, and spoiled everything, converting what had appeared a certain triumph into a disastrous failure. If the horses had only happened to touch land ten feet further up or ten feet further down, where the bank was less steep, by this time we might have been on the road to Sandy Point. But everything seemed to be against us. I had brought all my energy to this last attempt, the last chance of reaching our destination in time for the steamer of the 1st November. It had failed, and I felt unmanned and dispirited. My physical strength, too, was giving way under these repeated exertions and the poor diet of the last two weeks.

All these considerations combined, and there being no immediate necessity for crossing the river now, as the next steamer did not leave Sandy Point till the 10th November, made us resolve to wait a few days longer before risking another attempt at swimming over, especially as all this time the water had been rapidly decreasing again; and, judging by the height of the river, we might now reasonably expect to find it fordable in, at most, three or four days, always supposing that no new flood occurred. We had, therefore, merely to closely watch the river, so as to be ready to cross again, if any signs of a fresh rise should appear.

Notwithstanding that we were now well into spring, I was surprised to find but little corresponding change in the weather. Occasionally we had a warm day, but it was the exception, and was sure to be immediately followed by unusual cold. The west wind blew almost unintermittingly, and always with extreme violence. In fact, with all my memories of Patagonia are closely associated, as one of the most prominent peculiarities of its landscapes, the fiercely cold but exhilarating blasts of that same wild west wind. But though the weather had got but little warmer, there was everywhere a marked change in the vegetation. The grass in the glens was gradually becoming fresh and green, and the bright young leaves of the calafaté bush were interspersed with bunches of small yellow flowers. Flowers, too—red and white orchids, and pink cowslips—were springing up amongst the grass; and that none of the associations of springtime might be wanting, clouds of tiny little swallows, white-breasted and with glittering blue wings—come from Heaven knows where—were to be seen skimming through the air in all directions. Wretched and miserable indeed must be the spot over which spring can pass without making her genial influence felt in some way, though it be but in the transitory brightening of a few poor blades of grass.

It is fortunate that the calafaté is everywhere abundant in Patagonia, as its wood affords excellent fuel, being extremely hard and burning very slowly. At night-time we would cover up the embers well, and were sure to find them still smouldering in the morning, and were thus able to economize our matches, of which we had now but few left.

The valley had become the rendezvous of wild fowl of all descriptions,—swans, wild geese, ducks, snipe, etc.; and many a time we regretted not having brought a gun with us. A roast goose now and then would have made a welcome improvement on our eternal diet of lean guanaco and ostrich. A bevy of ibis, or "bandurria," as the Chilians call them, used to make a point every evening of assembling close to our camp, and lifting up their voices and quacking till an hour or so after sundown. Their note resembles that of the duck, though it is rather shorter and drier. They seemed to know, confound them! that they had nothing to fear from us, and would let us come quite near enough to enable us to see how provokingly fat they all were. The Indians call the wild geese of those parts, "kay-kén," in imitation of its cry, which has a rather melancholy sound, and which was always sounding in our ears, morning, noon, and evening, repeated by a thousand throats in lengthened and mournful cadences. All these wild fowl remain in the southern valleys till their young are fledged, and then as the warm weather comes on they fly north, and play havoc among the rich corn-fields of the Rio Negro.

Two days went by, and we began to find ourselves running short of meat, our stock having only been calculated to last for four days, as we had made our provision on the assumption of reaching Sandy Point by that time. It was, therefore, necessary for Guillaume to go back to Isidoro to fetch the dogs. As it was a long distance, being more than 120 miles there and back, and being anxious to spare our horses as much as possible, we first went out to see if we could hunt up a puma, the only animal one can kill without the aid of dogs,— the bolas or a revolver being all that is required.

But after a long search we were unsuccessful, and early the next morning, therefore, Guillaume started off, leaving a small piece of meat which was to last me till the evening of the next day, by which time he hoped to be back.

When he was gone, I saddled my horse and rode up the Cañada of the Squaws to collect firewood, as there was none near our camp. I found it no easy task to break off the dry branches out of thorny bushes, or pull up old roots which were firmly seated in the ground, in my present weak state, and I was glad when I had got sufficient wood to last me for that and the following day. At no period of my sojourn in Gallegos had I felt so weak as I now did. For three days we had eaten next to nothing—in fact, less than I could ordinarily eat myself at one meal—and I have already said how little sustaining power there is even in a large quantity of lean guanaco or ostrich meat.

When I got back to the camp, I cooked a small piece of the meat Guillaume had left me, and then carefully deposited it on the top of one of the walls of the house, so as to be out of reach of the foxes, who are terrible marauders, and who will eat your reins, lasso, saddle even, or any leathern article you may be so incautious as to leave lying about.

Feeling tired, after my frugal meal, which compared to my hunger was but as a drop in the ocean, I lay down on my furs and dosed off into a sound sleep, from which I was presently awakened by a confusion of strange screeches and flapping of wings. Starting up, I found the noise proceeded from some carranchos, who were quarrelling over my meat, or rather over the bone, which was all that I found of it, after I had driven them away with stones and strong language. "*Incidit in Scyllam*," etc. In my endeavours to secure my food from the foxes, I had delivered it into the beaks and claws of the carranchos, and felt not a little annoyed at my own carelessness. It was no pleasant matter having to fast for the next thirty hours, hungry as I already was, and if Guillaume by some possible accident were detained a day longer, I might find myself in a very serious plight. I was evidently out of luck, and that with a vengeance, and I began to wonder what my next mishap would be. The only misfortune that could now happen to me was that my horse might take it into his head to run away, and then I should indeed be in a desperate fix. He was quietly grazing at the time, but the idea of such a possibility so startled me that I immediately tied a lasso to his halter and secured it to a huge stone near the house, so as to prevent any such untoward eventuality. Then, feeling hungry, I commenced to search my traps for any stray piece of meat that might possibly have been forgotten there. All I could find was a small piece of puma fat, wrapped up in a piece of linen, in a coat-pocket of Guillaume's, which had doubtless been intended for greasing the dogs' paws when wounded, for which purpose it is considered an excellent specific. To me, under my present circumstances, however, it was quite a treasure, and I immediately cooked and ate half, keeping the rest for the next day.

Having made all my arrangements for passing the night, I made a good fire, as it was very cold, and wrapping myself up well in my capa, I sat down beside it, waiting as stoically as I could for night time, and trying to forget, amidst the splendour of the sunset, the small sharp whisper of the little voice within my stomach.

From the slight elevation where I was now sitting I could overlook the whole of the surrounding country—the far hills and plains; the winding valley shut in by steep cliffs, past whose base the river swept its tortuous course; the broad lakes formed by the overflow of its waters, dotted everywhere with green islands, where thousands of wild fowl were now assembled,—the harsh cries of the gulls and the plaintive note of the kay-kén being the only sounds that broke the otherwise intense silence. Over all the setting sun was pouring his last rays, bathing the distant hills in a warm haze, and burnishing the waters at my feet with fiery showers of light, and lending, with his magic tints of red and gold, a transitory gleam of grace and beauty, even to that wild desert spot.

But as the sun went down the charm sped with him. The glory departed from the distant hills, and they became grey and cold as before; the light faded from the valley, the waters assumed a muddy hue, and the islands blackened on their surface. The cry of the wild fowl slowly ceased, and below me, soon, all was silent and dark.

The stars crept out one by one, and still I sat by the red gleams of the dying fire, listening to the whispering voices of the night wind and watching the weird, ghostly shapes occasionally assumed by the white mist that now hung over the valley, as it swayed mysteriously to and fro, like a band of unquiet spirits.

The whole thing seemed so unreal, the turn of events so fantastic, which had brought me, a child of noisy towns and bustling marts, into my strange position, alone in that immense solitude—the wildness of the scene, starlit and dim, the strange noises of the night, the thousand sounds which yet seemed silence—I thought it must all be a dream, and most surely I must awaken and find myself in my own room, under warm bedclothes, with the voice of the servant with my shaving water ringing in my ears.

But a shiver of cold which went through my body, and the strong pangs of hunger, were quite sufficient to remind me of the reality of all around me; so, heaping some more wood on the fire and giving another look to see if the horse was secure, I sought my couch, to sleep as best I might till morning.

A sharp frost fell during the night, much to my satisfaction, as I had now strong hopes of crossing the river in a couple of days. Having satisfied myself that the water was still falling rapidly—always my first task of a morning—I cooked and ate the remaining piece of puma fat, and then, still feeling terribly hungry, and as a means of killing time till Guillaume should come, I tried to stalk wild geese with my revolver. I could never come within range, however, though they are not very shy, and finally gave up this unexciting and unproductive sport in a rather unpleasant state of mind, as I began to ask myself what I should do if Guillaume should happen not to come back that day.

Casting my eyes about, they happened to fall on a large island in the middle of the valley, which had often attracted our attention on account of its being the rendezvous of a bevy of swans, which we imagined must have nests and eggs there, and we had often meditated a raid on the latter. Hitherto we had been hindered from doing so, because the island was surrounded for a long distance by very deep water, which, as may be imagined, was quite sufficient to keep the swans' eggs safe from us as long as anything else could be found to eat. Since we had last surveyed the defences of the island, however, the water had fallen very much, and it occurred to me, in my present stress, that by carefully searching I might find a tolerably dry road to the island. I accordingly saddled my horse, and set out on my exploration. After a great deal of splashing and several narrow escapes of tumbling into holes, varied by occasional energetic protests from my horse—who, by-the-by, after all his late experience and his daily three or four rides through the water to examine the river, must have thought I was trying to convert him into an amphibious animal—I at last managed to discover a route which was almost practicable, and which by the next day, when the water would have fallen still further, would probably be thoroughly so. I could distinctly see several swans sitting on their nests, to whom I waved a light *au revoir*, and then returned to the camp, feeling that even if Guillaume were not to come back that day, I now knew where to find my dinner, although at the expense of a slight wetting.

However, I fortunately had no necessity for incurring that inconvenience; for, towards five o'clock, just as—despairing of his return—I was getting ready to swim over to the island, I descried him galloping towards the camp. He presently arrived, bringing the dogs, some meat, and four ostrich's eggs he had found on the way.

Famished as I was after my long fast, I lost no time in spitting some meat and setting it to roast, busying myself whilst it was cooking with the preparation of an ostrich's egg *à la Patagonienne*. The process is as follows: You break a small round hole in the top of the egg, and after having removed some of the white, which is rather heavy for the stomach, and having thoroughly beaten up the yolk, you set the egg on its end in the ashes, at a little distance from the fire, carefully turning it now and then to prevent the shell from cracking. Whilst cooking, it must occasionally be removed from the fire, and the batter must be stirred well, or else it will stick to the sides of the shell and burn. In a quarter of an hour it will be well roasted; add pepper and salt, if you have any, and serve. Our stock of these useful condiments had unfortunately long been exhausted. Cooked in this way, ostriches' eggs are excellent, and far better than when boiled. The act of removing and placing them near the fire whilst roasting, requires great nimbleness of finger. I had, during my noviciate, two standing sores or burns on forefinger and thumb, as I would sometimes cook as many as three or four eggs a day. They are held to be very indigestible, two eggs eaten in a day being said to endanger a man's life; but the foregoing is a proof to the contrary. I have known Guillaume to eat six eggs in the space of eight hours, independent of his ordinary meals. It is true his powers were beyond the usual run, even of those of his own habits and profession.

In the conversation which ensued, when I had in some degree allayed the pangs of hunger, Guillaume told me that on his way down he had paid a flying visit to the Middle Pass, the result of which was that he considered it the best place to cross over, in case, contrary to our present expectations, we should again be obliged to swim for it. The banks on the other side were all low-lying, and there would consequently be no danger of a repetition of the accident which had prevented us from crossing over at the pass we were now at. In return for this information, I told him of my discovery of a road to the island; and, eggs being almost indispensable to us for keeping up our failing strength, for which the meat alone was quite inadequate, we resolved to make a raid on the nests the following morning.

Shortly after daybreak, therefore, we set out towards the island, each of us armed with a stick and a revolver, in case the birds, which are said to be very savage, should think fit to resent our seizure of their eggs. The road to the island was not as favourable as it had appeared to me the day before, and we got soaked up to the waist in crossing over; but, in the excitement of the chase, we took little notice of that. Long before we arrived, a commotion was visible amongst the inmates of the island; several male swans, and crowds of wild geese and other fowl, flew up and hovered over us, watching our onward course with signs of marked disapproval. The female birds, however, kept their seats till we were within ten yards of them, and then rose with a hissing cry and much flapping of wings, circling over our heads, and occasionally gliding close to us, whilst we were despoiling their nests, though without making any attempt at attacking us. We found eight swans' nests, containing each four eggs, besides some forty wild geese's eggs. To mitigate the distress of the birds, we left one egg in each nest, and with the rest of our booty returned to the camp in triumph. Whilst our wet clothes were drying by the fire, wrapped in our capas, we set to and commenced roasting some swans' eggs. They are about half the size of ostriches' eggs, and of a similar taste. Amongst the other eggs were some of a species of duck, which to my taste seemed incomparably finer than the best bantam's, and, as may be imagined, we were not slow in doing full justice to them.

At five o'clock I mounted my horse, and rode leisurely towards the river, as was my habit, in order to watch the progress of its gradual decrease, which, as I have already said, had been very satisfactory lately. But to-night, already from afar I was startled by the appearance of the banks, which seemed to me lower than usual. The mark confirmed my fears. The water had risen more than two inches. In deep dismay I galloped back to the camp, and told Guillaume the bad news. For a moment the blow left us bewildered. Experience had taught us that one night would suffice to flood the river as high as it had been before. It seemed as if we were again to be thrown back a fortnight. It was time to adopt some decisive measures. Late as it was, I suggested that we should ride off that very night to the Middle Pass, and swim across at daybreak, be the river as it might. There was no time to lose in indecision, and half an hour after I proposed this plan, we had packed up our things, saddled the horses, and were once more on the march. The sun was setting as we emerged from Gallegos valley into the plain, and before long it was quite dark. It was midnight when we arrived at the old camp at the Middle Pass, cold and blue, after a long buffeting with our old enemy, the wind. Tired as we were, we had to collect wood to make a fire with, in order to warm ourselves by, before we could get to sleep.

XII

A DESPERATE SWIM

THE morning broke, as it always did whenever we tried to cross the river, bleakly and coldly. The river had risen considerably during the night, and was still rising rapidly. Previous to our other arrangements, we fixed on a site from which to start ourselves, after the horses should once be safely across.

The chief danger in passing the river lay in the possibility of the middle current being too strong for us to stem, in which case we should of necessity be swept along with it, without being able to reach either bank, until, our strength giving way under the combined influence of the cold and our exertions, we should ultimately perish. The spot we chose seemed to obviate this danger, as a little way down the opposite bank made a broad curve, forming a point which shot for a long way into the river. I could see that the current followed the curve, running inside the point. By committing ourselves, therefore, to the current at some distance above the point, we must of necessity, I argued, bring up in the little bay formed by the curve above mentioned, in which case the point would act as an effectual bar to our being swept down the centre of the river. All this seemed plausible enough; but we were reckoning without our host, however, as I presently discovered, and in ignorance of the course taken by the current, which did not, as we supposed, always follow the bend of the banks or keep in the centre of the river, where the water was deepest, but darted about capriciously, without apparently depending on any topographical influences, though no doubt it did.

We first made a large fire near the river, to warm ourselves by whilst packing and saddling the horses, so that the caloric of our bodies should not be all exhausted, as on the last occasion, before we had to make the final struggle, when we should have most need of it. It proved a most providential act; this same fire subsequently saved my life. We made our preparations in deep silence, being both too busy with our own thoughts to say much. We were firmly resolved that, *coûte que coûte*, this was to be our last effort. We had the usual difficulty to induce the horses to enter the water. Once in, however, they were soon seized by the current and swept down the river. We watched their course with the most intense anxiety. At first it seemed that they could not stem the current, which was evidently stronger than it had been at our last attempt. For a moment we held our breath in painful suspense, but gradually they began to gain towards the opposite bank, and presently we saw them emerge safe and sound from the water, though the distance they had been carried down showed what the strength of the current must be.

Everything now depended on ourselves. The supreme moment had come, and not a second was to be lost, for already I began to feel numb with the cold. On the other side were our clothes, our furs, our matches,—our existence, in fact. Between us lay the river. We must cross it; there was no alternative. I ran as quickly as possible towards the place we had chosen for starting from, not daring to look at the river on the way, lest my courage should fail me now that I most required its aid. I had to wade for some distance through a sheet of shallow water before reaching the river itself. It only came up to my waist, which made it colder than if I had been completely immersed, and the wind was piercing all the time to the very marrow of my bones. Suddenly I fell into a hole, sousing head over ears into the water. Chilled and breathless with the shock, I emerged after a short swim, and hurried on my way, anxious to get it all over. At last I came to the river. Without pausing a moment, I jumped in, with a feeling of relief that the worst would now soon be passed. I struck out with the current, and, as I had foreseen, it swept me rapidly towards the point. In a few seconds I was close to the bank. I stretched out my hands to clutch at the grass, when, to my horror, the land seemed suddenly to recede from me again. The current had swerved off before actually reaching land, and I was being hurried with fearful swiftness into the middle of the river. I tried to make for land, but my legs and arms stiffened, and I seemed to be dragged under the water. A desperate struggle brought me once more to the surface. I remember catching a glimpse of the blue sky, and feeling with sickening terror that I was lost, and again I sank under.

For a second or two I think I must have been unconscious; when I came to myself again, I felt I was in warmer water. My strength revived a little, and I struck out several times towards a bank, close along which I was being hurried in the direction of another point a little further down. At times I came so near the bank that I could actually stretch out my hands and reach the long grass growing on it, but my fingers, stiffened with the cold, refused to close on what alone could save me from being swept away again. It was a horrible moment, for if I passed the next point, I was indeed lost. I shouted for help, but no one answered; it almost seemed that I was to be drowned with one foot on land, so to speak.

Suddenly, however, my feet touched the bottom, and in another second, carried bodily against the extremity of the point, I found myself in shallow water, where I was able to regain my footing, and take breath once more. I managed to drag myself up the bank; but on reaching the top, my strength gave way again, and, overcome with cold and fatigue, I sank down, utterly prostrate and helpless. On emerging from the river, a glance had shown me that ill luck had willed that I should be thrown up on the same side from which I had started. Fortunately, I found myself not far distant from the fire we had made before crossing, and with my remaining strength I now endeavoured to reach it. I could only breathe with the greatest difficulty; at times I thought I must choke. I tried to raise myself up and walk, but failed; my legs were like lead, all circulation seemed arrested, and I could only crawl slowly along on all fours. Many times I thought I must give in, but with the energy of despair I struggled on, and at last reached the fire, which was still burning. Some logs of wood were lying close to it; I pushed them in, and there was soon a good blaze. It seemed to give me no warmth, however, though in my agony I almost thrust my body into the very flames. Nearly an hour elapsed before circulation was properly restored, during which I lay shivering with cold, and gasping for breath in a state of the most acute suffering.

When I had in some measure recovered, I began to realize the critical position I was now placed in. Terrible as the idea was to me after my recent narrow escape from drowning, I had no alternative but to attempt to cross the river again. If I remained where I was, certain death from starvation or exposure awaited me; and it was useless to endeavour to reach Isidoro, who was at least forty miles away, for, naked as I was, I could not have gone even half a mile upon the plains, in the teeth of the cold wind, which was, of course, still blowing. I had all this time thought it strange that Guillaume had not come to my assistance, as I had expected that he would have delayed crossing himself, until he had watched the result of my own attempt. That he had safely crossed, however, now became evident, for I could see the horses grazing unsaddled on the opposite side. Where he had crossed, there was no reason why I should not be able to follow, unless it was that he had swum over comparatively fresh and strong, whereas I had now hardly recovered from the effects of my first unsuccessful struggle.

It was at worst but a question of taking another plunge, and then a few seconds would decide one way or the other, and after all, sooner or later, I should be forced to cross, as it was simply impossible to remain where I was. It was better, therefore, I reflected, to go through the ordeal at once, rather than increase its terrors by long anticipation. Screwing up my courage, without more ado, I started off as quickly as I could, to look for the place Guillaume had started from. At this juncture he himself suddenly appeared on the opposite bank, and guessing my intention, ran forward and pointed the exact place out to me. It was much higher up than where I had started from, and to get to it, as before, I had to wade through some shallow water, which now and then was deep enough to oblige me to swim. When I reached the exact spot, I could easily see why he had chosen it—no doubt, after having witnessed my mishap—for the current ran almost straight across from where I stood to the other bank, where it broke with great force, so that there was no danger of my being swept away from the bank, as before, just as I got up to it. I had in fact, merely to jump in, and allow myself to be swept passively over by the current. Notwithstanding the apparent simplicity and easiness of the undertaking, I stood for some time looking at the water, with an instinctive dread, not daring to take the first step. A man who has just escaped drowning may be excused for fearing to trust himself, five minutes after, to the water again. But, feeling a chill come over my body, and apprehensive lest by further exposing myself to the air I should bring on a cramp, I nerved myself for the plunge, and, shutting my eyes and setting my teeth, I sprang into the water. Once in, all fear left me, and I struck out boldly and, aided by the current, soon reached the opposite shore.

My feelings on finding myself in safety on the Sandy Point side of the river may be imagined. All the hardships I had endured, the reverses I had suffered, the dangers I had undergone—all was forgotten in the triumphant elation of that moment; the fatal obstacle which had so long retarded our onward march was at last overcome, and there was nothing to prevent us now from speedily arriving at our destination.

Meanwhile I staggered through the band of shallow water which still separated me from Guillaume, who was waiting for me with a dry capa. With the support of his arm, I managed to reach a fire he had made at a little distance from the water, and there I covered myself with three capas, which restored the warmth to my body quicker than a thousand fires could have done.

In about half an hour I was sufficiently recovered to eat an ostrich steak, and to listen to Guillaume's account of what had happened to him since we had last seen each other. He had watched the course of my ill-fated attempt, had seen me struggling for life in the water, and at last disappear altogether; after which, as he had not seen me return, he had naturally concluded I was drowned. But his own safety required that he should not linger any longer, or the horses, finding themselves left to their own devices, might take it into their heads to run away with the furs and clothes. It was clear, too, that he must not commit the same error in the selection of his starting-point as had brought me into difficulties, and he had, therefore, followed the course of the river till he came to the spot I have already described, and which, as the result proved, possessed the necessary requirements for insuring his safety. Naturally enough, with the demoralizing impressions of what he had just witnessed in my case fresh in his mind, he was not without some unpleasant misgivings as to the eventual result of his own attempt. He had crossed with ease, however, and it was in going to look after the horses that he saw me in the act of creeping towards the fire on the other side. He certainly had not thought I should have strength enough to cross the river again, and had been very much troubled about me, not knowing in what way to assist me. In the mean time he had made a good fire, and with the aid of the wind and sun, which latter had at last come from behind the clouds, he had thoroughly dried our clothes and furs, and was just considering what could be done to relieve me from my perilous plight, when he observed me running along the opposite shore, with the obvious intention of once more trying to swim across.

By this time it was about half-past two, and, burning with the desire to accomplish my journey, I proposed we should continue our march immediately as we might still go a good way on our road before sundown. I accordingly dressed; we saddled our horses, and soon rode out of the valley up to the plain, turning as we reached the top of the escarpment which bounded the valley, to have a last look on our vanquished enemy, the river—now, thank God, at last behind us—and then, facing towards the south-west, we broke into a brisk gallop, once more *en route* for Sandy Point.

XIII

A SERIOUS LOSS

WE presently came to a hilly country, where the plains were of shorter duration, and cut up in all directions by steeper and more irregular cañadas than I had hitherto met; whilst occasionally we passed broad tracts of scoriæ which forced us, in consideration of our horses, to change our gallop for a soberer pace. These tracts grew more and more frequent as we approached a range of high hills, at whose base we hoped to camp that night, though as yet their jagged and fantastic outlines showed but dimly on the distant horizon.

We passed several herds of guanacos, who fled away at our approach. Presently, however, one solitary animal, whose curiosity was stronger than its good sense, came neighing and frisking around us, halting at last almost under our very noses. The voice of his master had hitherto kept back our remaining dog (the other had refused to cross the river); but this was rather more than he could stand, and darting out from behind our horses, where he had hitherto very unwillingly kept himself, he flew out at the startled guanaco, who, on seeing him, gave an affrighted bound, and stretched away over the plain with the speed of lightning. The dog followed pretty close on its heels. Our blood was up, and we dashed after them as fast as the horses would carry us, to aid the dog in case he should turn the guanaco round our way. For a moment they ran pretty evenly, but then the guanaco, evidently a tough old male, gradually distanced his pursuer, though the latter was a remarkably swift dog, and of very good breed. We were just despairing of the chase, when it suddenly became apparent that the guanaco was in difficulties, his flight having been arrested by a belt of marshy ground, where his heavy weight immediately put him at a great disadvantage. The very efforts he made to redouble the force of his bounds only caused his sharp hoofs to sink deeper into the heavy soil; and in a few seconds the dog, whose speed was not so much affected by the nature of the ground, had reached his now helpless prey, and flown at its throat. We soon came up to them, and Guillaume, dismounting, despatched the guanaco with his long hunting-knife.

After all, the game turned out to be not worth the candle, or rather the sunlight we had lost in its pursuit, for it proved to be as lean of flesh as it had been swift of foot. We, therefore, merely stayed to cut off and secure its head, and then resumed our journey with all speed, as the sun was already getting low, and we had still a long ride before us. Fate, however, seemed determined to prevent us reaching our intended halting-place that night. Not long after the guanaco-hunt an ostrich started up, so close to us that Guillaume could not resist the temptation, but went off in its pursuit, whilst I looked about for the nest. I found it to contain fourteen eggs, which I carefully packed up so that they should not break, and then rode off to meet Guillaume, who I was glad to see had the ostrich already dangling at his saddle. It turned out to be tolerably fat, which, considering the season, was quite a miracle. This piece of fortune put us into high spirits, and, as we remarked to each other, our bad luck had evidently abandoned us at last.

On we rode, gradually getting nearer to the hills, which now loomed blackly against the sky; for the sun had already sunk behind their sharp, irregular peaks, and night was coming on apace. We passed several large lakes, which proved to be salt,—and gloomy and dismal they looked, encircled by broad belts of shingle and sand, with not a single bush or blade of grass in their blighting vicinity. Leaving them behind us, we stumbled on over the lava-covered ground, across a wild-looking plain, strewn with jagged masses of rock, through which our horses picked their way with extreme difficulty. The ruggedness of the country increased as we proceeded, and when we at last came to a break, where there was a small plain with plenty of grass and a pool of fresh water, we resolved to go no further, but to remain there for the night.

We brought our saddles and traps to a clump of stones, which made a good shelter against the wind, and then hobbled one of the horses, and secured the other with a long cord to a heavy stone,—a precaution not absolutely necessary, as after a hard day's work they do not care to stray far, but which we thought better to take on this occasion, as we were in a broken country, where we might have a great deal of difficulty in finding them again, even if they only strayed a couple of hundred yards. Having made our minds easy on this point, we set about preparing supper, which, with the abundance of material at our disposal, was an easy and a grateful task. We were altogether in the very best of spirits that evening, under the influence of our unwonted good cheer, and at the thoughts of our speedy arrival at Sandy Point and the indulgencies we should then be able to allow ourselves in such long-missed luxuries as coffee, sugar, bread, tobacco, etc., of which and similar dainties we talked till our mouths watered again. We reviewed the events of the day, too, and recounted the various impressions and feelings they had given rise to. It was an open question who had passed the worst *quart d'heure*—I whilst struggling in the water and feeling that all was over, or Guillaume, when, after he had seen me disappear without returning, he reflected that he must run the same risk, and possibly incur the same fate. Meanwhile, having roasted and eaten as many eggs as we dared, we sought our couches and, overcome by our day's exertions, soon fell into a sound sleep.

The words with which Guillaume woke me in the morning brushed the sleepiness from my brain in an instant, and made me jump to my feet and stare blankly about me in utter dismay. "The horses have stampeded!" I said, repeating the sentence slowly after him, dwelling on each word in complete stupefaction. He nodded his head dejectedly, and sank down on his couch, and for a long time neither of us spoke, each giving way to his own gloomy train of thought.

It was, indeed, a stroke of misfortune, which, happening as it did on the very night after we had overcome what we believed to be the only obstacle which separated us from Sandy Point, appeared almost in the light of an intimation that we were fated never to reach our destination.

The idea took such firm hold of my mind, and so completely paralyzed my energy, that for a short space I allowed myself to give way to despair, and to a feeling of incapacity to struggle any longer against what in my agitation appeared to me a superior decree of destiny. In truth, the difficulties which beset us were no ordinary ones. We were about 150 miles from Sandy Point— no great distance to walk, it is true, for a strong, healthy man, who can depend on a supply of proper nourishment. But we were so weakened that even such a slight exertion as saddling our horses seemed often too much for our strength; the effort required for crossing the river had been a spasmodic burst, which we were quite incapable of sustaining for any length of time. Besides, we were wholly unaccustomed to walking, and long inaction had relaxed those muscles we now most required. Even then, however, it was not so much the actual distance which frightened me as the nature of the ground to be gone over. There were streams to be crossed, which at that time of the year could be swollen and perhaps impassable for us; marshy grounds to be traversed, which to a man on horseback were nothing, but to cross which on foot implied continual wettings; and we had only four matches left, and therefore no means of making a fire to dry ourselves by when once these were used. Taking the uncongenial season into consideration, we were not wrong in doubting whether our bodies would stand all these hardships. With proper food, no doubt, they would; but there was another great difficulty. When once we had consumed the ostriches' eggs and the meat we had left, how were we to procure more? We had a dog, it is true; but how could we follow him on foot, when, in a few minutes, he could pursue a guanaco for ten miles, and run his prey to earth somewhere, far beyond our ken? Besides, within a certain distance from Sandy Point the guanacos cease altogether, and ostriches are very scarce. The Indians, Guillaume knew, were somewhere near the colony. We might, therefore, meet them on the road, in which case we should be all right; but, on the other hand, they might have struck towards the Cordilleras, which certainly would have been more in keeping with our general luck. Whatever happened, one thing was certain, and that was that we had a great deal of misery and hardship to face, even supposing we should have strength to overcome all difficulties and reach our destination in safety.

All these considerations passed through my mind in rapid succession, but having once looked the situation steadily in the face and contemplated it in all its bearings, my courage rose again, and I felt it was a great deal too soon to despair. After all, there are very few difficulties that are not to be vanquished by determination, and, my momentary fit of despondency over, I nerved myself to face whatever new trials might be in store for us.

Guillaume now told me how he had risen at daybreak and found the horses gone, the cord which had tied one of them being broken. Amongst the confused tracks he had seen footmarks of a puma, a circumstance which led him to suppose that this animal must have frightened the horses during the night and caused them to stampede. He followed the tracks for a great distance, and then lost them in a plain of scoriæ, where it was, of course, impossible to trace them any further. As a last chance, he had climbed several hills and overlooked the surrounding country, without, however, being able to see the horses anywhere; and at last, completely exhausted, he had returned to the camp. Having rapidly reviewed our position, we resolved to commence our pilgrimage immediately, as time was precious, in view of the poor state of our larder. Not a moment was to be lost—not on account of catching the steamer; that was no longer uppermost in my mind—but we must now hurry over as much ground as possible daily, to save our lives.

I rolled two of my capas tightly together, and strapped them on my shoulders like a knapsack. Guillaume took a capa and a pair of saddle-bags, in one side of which he put the six remaining eggs, and in the other all that was left of the ostrich, which was not much after our supper of last night and what we had given to the dog, for the bird, though fat, had unfortunately been small. With as strict an economy as was compatible with keeping up our strength, we had enough provisions to last us for four days; after that—well, *quien sabe;* but I had resolutely made up my mind not to think of the future, so all was right—for the present. We took our knives, of course, and one tin cup; our revolvers, as being too heavy, we left behind us, as well as our saddles, beds, superfluous clothes, etc., etc., for the benefit of the foxes, or whoever should chance to find them.

XIV

A CHANGE IN LUCK

WE started off in tolerably good spirits, and it was well we did so, for we had to draw upon them considerably before the day was over. Our way lay over a short plain, and across the range of hills above mentioned. For the first two miles all went well, but after we had climbed a couple of hills, I began to feel distressed. My burden, which at the commencement had weighed lightly enough, now began seriously to incommode me, and I asked myself, if my strength was already giving way before the journey had hardly begun, how was I to reach its end? Still, with closed teeth and bent brow, I dragged myself wearily along, determined not to give in. Guillaume was in no better plight than I. We had long since abandoned any attempt at conversation—it only used up our precious breath, and tired us the more.

At last we had to halt and rest a little, starting off again after a few minutes' breathing time, till we were again obliged to stop to collect our strength; and in this manner we went on all that afternoon, panting up steep hills, and dragging ourselves along over plains which succeeded each other in weary monotony, and where the boisterous winds, blowing full against us, obliged us to double our exertions. At each fresh start we made I had to put forth my whole strength to nerve myself for the effort, and each time, I felt, would surely be the last. Somehow or other, I kept on, however. It is wonderful what one can do in the face of certain alternatives. I soon suffered from another cause; my feet, tender from long disuse, began to swell under these sudden exertions. I was unable, after suffering for some time, to keep my boots on, and had to continue the march barefooted, over pebbles and sharp grasses which were only slightly less merciless than the boots had been.

At sunset we found ourselves descending into a valley, where there was a small river. We had fortunately no necessity to cross it, as our road lay along the valley itself. In this region, the bushes, which had gradually been getting scarcer, ceased altogether. In the country we were about to traverse, you may ride for leagues and leagues without being able to find a piece of wood big enough to make a toothpick with. The Indians, when they pass through this region, always bring sufficient firewood with them on their pack-horses to last them during the transit. I can in no way account for the absence in that particular region of the bushes peculiar to the rest of the country, especially as the soil, the formation, and the atmospheric conditions seem to be the same there as in the rest of Patagonia.

By the time we had gone a little way up the valley we were all but completely exhausted; my legs felt like lead, my breath came with difficulty, and I staggered along as if about to fall at every step under my pack, whose weight seemed to increase almost at every step. It soon became necessary for us to halt altogether. We threw off our burdens and stretched ourselves on the grass, to enjoy the luxury of a good rest before troubling ourselves about getting supper ready.

But this important task could not be long deferred, especially as it was getting dark. We therefore began to cast about for some substitute for firewood, of which, as I have already mentioned, there was absolutely none in that region. Guillaume consolingly remarked that as soon as our four matches were exhausted, we should have to eat our meat raw, and might as well, therefore, begin to do so at once. I was not of his opinion, however, feeling that the longer that unpleasant necessity was deferred, the better. The only suitable combustible we were able to find was the dry dung of guanacos, of which we managed to collect a good heap. We purposed to ignite it with some dry grass, but as we only allowed ourselves one match that day, I trembled for the result. Carefully sheltering it from the wind, the match was at length struck in safety and applied to the grass. It blazed up quick enough, but it had to be fed some time before the dung could be coaxed into taking fire, or rather smouldering, for the flame it emitted was almost imperceptible. With the aid of the wind, the glow gradually spread itself over the whole heap, and in it we managed to roast our eggs and even to cook some meat. The latter had a disagreeable flavour, even to our hardened palates. As soon as we finished our supper, we lost no time in getting under our capas, now our only bed, as the fire held out but few enticements to linger over it longer than was absolutely necessary for cooking purposes.

At daybreak the next morning we got up, and in the heap of dung, which was fortunately still glowing, we cooked some eggs and prepared for starting. I wrapped some pieces of cloth round my feet, to protect them from hurt, and then we saddled ourselves and continued the march. I felt very stiff, and altogether thoroughly done up. In fact, I did not think I should be able to go on for more than a couple of hours at most. Our path still lay through the valley, alongside the river, and we had now come to the beaten track to Sandy Point, made in the course of long years by the Indians on their annual visit to that settlement.

Here we were pleasantly surprised by the sudden apparition of a big dog, who frisked and jumped about us in great glee, no doubt glad to have met with human beings. He probably belonged to some Indian, and had lost himself somehow in the pursuit of a guanaco, as frequently happens.

This was the first gleam of sunshine after our late bad luck, for the poor brute was very fat, and we foresaw that its flesh would prove a godsend, if we should not happen to fall in with Indians. Our own dog was not worth killing, being merely skin and bone. In view of his probable fate, we called the new-comer "Infeliz,"—a name to which he soon got to answer. He became quite attached to me, little knowing why I paid him such anxious attentions.

We went on pretty well for some time; of course, with the usual halts every ten minutes. To-day, too, the weather took it into its head to change; the sun became unpleasantly warm, which, of course, increased our fatigue considerably. At about twelve o'clock the path broke off from the valley, and the country assumed a threatening appearance, hill rising above hill for a long distance. As we had walked more than six hours already, we allowed ourselves a long rest before facing the difficulties which now lay before us. We felt very hungry, too; but, not daring to use a match, we were obliged to eat some raw ostrich meat. I thought it had a peculiarly revolting taste, and more than ever I deprecated the idea of perhaps having to undergo a regimen of uncooked meat. I wondered, too, how Infeliz would taste raw, and felt that I certainly would not try him, unless pushed to the very last extremity.

When we felt somewhat restored, we arose, carefully collected the fragments of our meal, and then continued our wearisome journey. The path now lay across a succession of hills, or undulations, which were very steep and told fearfully upon us. We would rest a while on the crest of each, and then go at the next one with a rush, our teeth set and eyes bent on its summit; for if we flinched

once on our upward course, or halted but a moment, we were done for, and
had to take another rest, previous to collecting our strength for a new spurt.
Several times I thought I must give in, and at last I could literally hardly move
one leg before the other. The perspiration rolled off my forehead in streams,
and the weight of my capas seemed to break my back. Still we had set ourselves
a certain goal, which was yet a long way off; and though I was inwardly wishing
that Guillaume would give in, I was determined not to be first to speak, but
to go on as long as he did, whilst there was a step left in me. I believe he was
in the same plight as I was, but kept on for the same reasons. At last a higher
hill than usual fairly brought us to a regular standstill, and we threw ourselves
down, feeling that, for that day at least, we could go no further.

We lay motionless for about half an hour, when I rose to take off my pack,
and in so doing perceived a column of smoke, not far, at least to all appearance,
from where we were. My shout of joyful surprise brought Guillaume to his
feet, and we both examined it for some time, half doubting our own eyes, and
fearful lest every moment it should prove a delusion. Nor were our feelings of
pleasure wholly unmitigated by certain apprehensions that it might be some
old fire that had been lit two or three days ago, and which was now burning
up again. Guillaume told me that he had known fires to smoulder on in grassy
glens for weeks together. It might be but an hour old, and yet those who had
made it were, perhaps, already miles away in some direction, far from the path
we must follow; and we could not signal our own whereabouts, as the country
we were then crossing was bare of grass and bushes. Our doubts, however,
were speedily set at rest. Even as we watched the first column with eager eyes,
another rose up not far from it, and another still, and then we knew that the
fires were being made by Indians, who were hunting on the plains. A little to
the left of the smoke was a place called the "Campo de Batalla," where the
Indians always camp when in that neighbourhood, and to it we accordingly
directed our steps, as we were almost certain to find them there. The vicinity
of human beings gave us new strength. All fatigue disappeared as if by magic;
the hills, hitherto so formidable, seemed to shrink into pigmy mounds; my
pack became light as a feather, and the rags round my feet seemed suddenly
to possess the virtues of the famed seven-mile boots. Not only should we be
able to get horses from the Indians, but, as they must have recently left the
settlement, they would have plenty of tobacco, maté, sugar, and biscuit, with
the thought of which I charmed away any relapse into exhaustion, which, as
hill followed hill in endless succession, now and again threatened to overcome
me. At last, about four o'clock, we descended into a valley, a sudden turn of

which brought us in full view of the Indian encampment. My heart bounded at the sight of the tents, amongst which I could descry dark human figures in long robes, moving slowly to and fro; hundreds of horses were grazing in the valley, whilst the yelping of the swarms of curs that infest the Indian camps fell on my ears like pleasant music.

The Indians were just returning from the chase, and were pouring down from the plains on all sides. They soon perceived us, and presently fifty or more horsemen came flying towards us at full gallop. In another moment we were surrounded by a chattering, laughing, gesticulating crowd, who escorted us towards the camp in triumph. One of their number, who could speak a little Spanish, asked us a thousand questions, the answers to which he translated for the benefit of the others, to whom every item of information seemed to furnish an excuse for the most unbounded merriment; they would all giggle and laugh, though what I had to say to them did not contain anything extraordinarily funny, at least as far as my perception of the humorous goes.

When we reached the camp, we were surrounded by another crowd of Indians, as eagerly curious as the first comers to know where we came from, what we had done with our horses, and where we were going to,—in fact, all particulars as to our situation. As soon as one group left, another arrived; and in this manner we ran the gauntlet of the whole of the camp, every one apparently deeming it incumbent on him to come and have a good stare and grin at us.

Having satisfied their curiosity, we felt ourselves at liberty to consult our own comfort; and Guillaume having discovered the whereabouts of the tent of a cacique of the name of Orkeke, with whom he was on intimate terms, we directed our steps towards it. Orkeke himself we found, had not as yet returned from the chase; but his wife, an immensely fat and good-humoured looking old squaw, accosted us in some friendly gutturals, of which the evident purport was that we were to make ourselves at home—an intimation on which we speedily acted. With a deep sigh of relief I divested myself of the pack under whose weight I had trudged for so many a weary mile, and, stretching myself out on the ground, I inwardly congratulated myself that the unpleasant episode of our foot-pilgrimage was fortunately a thing of the past.

We had now, for the first time since we had seen the smoke, leisure to muse over our providential delivery from the serious danger that had threatened us,—a danger whose full magnitude only became apparent now that we had no longer to fear it. But these thoughts did not occupy us long; very soon Orkeke arrived, heavily laden with the spoils of the chase. He seemed very pleased to see us, and greeted us affably in broken Spanish. To the story of our mishaps he listened with great interest, and when I told him that I had not taken maté or smoked for several weeks, he showed particular concern, and immediately produced a pipe and tobacco, and bade me smoke, at the same time telling his wife to prepare maté, remarking very justly, "No fumar, no tomar maté; muy malo!" Smokers will feel with me when I say that my hand trembled whilst filling my pipe, and that, having lit it, I sat for a few minutes in a state of semi-ecstasy, enveloped in a fragrant cloud of the long-missed soul-soother. The maté, too, seemed delicious, and as a great treat, from a bag which contained similar treasures, Orkeke brought forth a musty biscuit, which he broke into three pieces, solemnly handing a share to Guillaume and me. The biscuit was coarse and black and hard, no doubt, but it melted away on my lips like a *meringue*, nor did I allow one crumb of it to be lost.

Orkeke was an admirable specimen of the Tehuelche race. He was tall and well proportioned, and, notwithstanding his great age, extremely vigorous and agile. His long grey hair and the benign expression of his face gave him the look of a venerable patriarch,—a character which he rather affected to maintain. He was careful to inform me, at an early stage of our acquaintance, that he never got drunk, like the other Indians; that he never told a lie; and that his father had been converted to Christianity,—a circumstance which he evidently considered to reflect in some way meritoriously on himself. On my asking him why he had not followed his father's example and become a Christian too, after a long pause he answered rather vaguely, "Quien sabe." I did not press the question any further, as the Indians who speak Spanish always make use of this expression when puzzled, or when they do not care to give a direct reply, and if once they proffer it as an answer, it is perfectly useless to attempt to elicit anything more explicit from them.

Orkeke told me that he remembered perfectly well having paid a visit to St. Julian, as a boy, when the Spanish colonists of Viedma were yet there. If that were true—and I have no reason to doubt his word—his age was now at least ninety-six or ninety-seven, and, judging by his looks, I thought he might easily live twenty or thirty years longer. His movements were as easy and as free from effort as those of a young man. Indeed, I should imagine few climates are healthier or more favourable to longevity than that of Patagonia; its crisp, dry air has a peculiarly beneficent effect both on mind and body, and under its influence one experiences a buoyancy of spirits, and a general well-being, which are quite astonishing.

Orkeke spoke Spanish with tolerable fluency, and I was able to have a long conversation with him on various topics, during which I gleaned some interesting information about the customs and thoughts of the Indians.

The tribe I was now amongst was more numerous than that of the Northern Tehuelches, but it seemed to me that they were, on the average, slightly inferior in physique to the Northerners, and certainly there were not so many pretty squaws among them as among the latter. Otherwise there was no marked distinction between them. The camp consisted of twelve tents, containing in all from four to five hundred souls. The whole tribe, I found, had just been paying their annual visit to Sandy Point, to receive the rations of sugar, biscuit, maté, and tobacco, which the Chilian Government accords them. These visits generally cost them rather dear, as the inhabitants of the colony, on these occasions, make a rich harvest of furs and feathers, with which, under the influence of aguadiente, the Indians are then extremely prodigal.

I made Orkeke promise to get me two horses the next morning, in order that we might immediately continue our journey, and having eaten a hearty supper, I went to sleep on a couch of furs, which Mrs. Orkeke had prepared for me, and, notwithstanding the incessant squalling of babies in various parts of the tent, I managed to pass a tolerable night.

The next morning, as soon as Orkeke had risen, I asked him to get the horses in readiness, as I was leaving at once. But there was an unpleasant surprise in store for me. Orkeke seemed to have no remembrance of what he had promised the previous evening, and coolly told me that he could not lend me any of his horses, as, according to him, they were all "thin and tired." "Mi caballo, muy flaco, muy cansado," was all I could get out of him in reply to my indignant demands for an explanation of the unaccountable change in his intentions. In vain I argued, entreated, and stormed; in vain I offered to pay him double the sum we had previously agreed on,—nothing would move him, and finally I gave up pressing the matter, directing my energies instead to discovering some more accommodating Indian.

My task was not an easy one, and I soon found out that to drive a bargain with an Indian one must have the patience of Job and the temper of an angel. It is next to an impossibility to get a plain "yes" or "no" out of them, as they have an insuperable aversion to committing themselves finally, either one way or the other. The consequence is that one may haggle with them for hours, without arriving at any result, and without even being able to judge whether one is likely to arrive at any, so vague and circumlocutory are their answers.

Unfortunately, too, I was obliged to employ an interpreter, thus reducing still further the chances of my coming to any definite understanding.

After having interviewed some forty Indians, who all, after more or less vacillation and delay, proffered the stereotyped objection, "Mi caballo, muy flaco," I began to despair of succeeding at all, and as a last resource, went back to Orkeke, who, I hoped, might possibly have again changed his mind and become less obdurate. But the obstinate old cacique was inexorable, and calmly recommended me to wait patiently for a few days, as very soon some traders would be coming from the colony. He could not understand that any one could possibly be in a hurry. Indians never are; and I have no doubt that the fact of my being in such a desperate haste to get away awoke some suspicions in his mind as to my motives, and inclined him to persist in his refusal to accommodate me. I was at my wits' end. Nothing could be further from my intentions than to wait with the Indians till some trader should come to the camp. The very thought made me furious. I had not risked crossing Gallegos for that, and yet I must either remain or start off on foot, neither of which prospects I contemplated with much satisfaction.

Though my own attempts had failed, I thought that perhaps Orkeke might be able to negotiate more successfully for the hire of two horses from some one amongst his acquaintances; and as an inducement for him to exert himself in my behalf, I offered to give him a guanaco mantle. My proposal set him thinking, and presently he said, "I know Indian—very rich man—three hundred horses—quien sabe, he lend you two." Of course, I jumped at the suggestion, and proposed that we should immediately go and see this great and good man, the owner of three hundred horses. But Orkeke met my impetuosity with a tantalizing "Mas tarde," and I had to restrain my impatience for more than an hour, during the course of which I relieved my feelings with many a bitter imprecation at Tehuelche supineness. At last Orkeke seemed to have nerved himself for the tremendous effort, and signified to me that he was ready to accompany me to the tent of the rich man. I approached this awful being, whom I found reclining at ease on his furs, with feelings of the deepest respect, for did he not hold the means of relieving me from the serious and aggravating plight which fate and the obstinacy of his brethren had brought me into?

Orkeke conversed with him for some time—very leisurely and unconcernedly, I thought, considering the gravity of the issue of the negotiations—and then, turning to me, he asked me to tell his friend, who understood Spanish, what I wanted.

I began. "You have plenty horses?"

"Yes, plenty."

"Quien sabe, you lend me two?"

Here a long pause, during which I anxiously endeavoured to read the answer to my question in the face of the Indian. But its expression was a blank. Presently he suggested—

"How much you pay?"

"Oh, plenty sugar, plenty biscuit, plenty silver dollar," I exclaimed, gesticulating to an unlimited extent, and radiant with satisfaction, as now I thought the matter had taken a practical and final turn.

"Bueno! But how send back horses to Indian?"

"Guillaume come back with horses and presents from colony in six days."

Here another long pause. The Indian seemed to be looking at some object on the hills, fifty miles away, apparently oblivious of my presence. As he did not offer to resume the conversation, after a while I suggested cheerfully—

"Very well, all is settled; you go and fetch the horses, whilst I prepare my things and get ready to leave." To my surprise he did not respond to my suggestion as readily as I had expected. I presumed I was going too quickly for him, and accordingly I modified my proposal this wise: "Quien sabe, when will you fetch horses for me ?"

No answer: the object on the hills still claimed his undivided attention. I waited patiently, wonderfully patiently, for a reply, though now and then, in the course of the quarter of an hour's silence which ensued, I did feel that it would have been an unspeakable relief to have given my nonchalant friend just one little cut with my whip. We cannot all have the dispositions of saints.

I contented myself, after the lapse of time mentioned, with repeating "Quien sabe, when will you fetch horses for me?"

Then fell on my ears "some words, which were warning of doom!"—" Mi caballo, muy flaco, muy cansado."

After having had my hopes raised to the highest point of expectation, to see them thus suddenly dashed to the ground, for some mere whim, and without a show of reason, was more than flesh and blood could stand; I regret to say that I lost my temper, and hurled at the passive Indian a shower of furious imprecations. I am bound to say, however, that they did not seem to have the slightest effect upon him, and merely provoked a chorus of mocking laughter from the squaws. I went away in a high dudgeon, and my reflections, after I had cooled down a little, were not rendered any pleasanter by the confession I had to make to myself, that I had no business to lose my temper, as, after all, the Indian had a perfect right to do as he chose with his own. Still, it was rather exasperating that, much as I wanted them, with two thousand horses grazing in the ravine around me, I could not obtain two.

Fortunately, relief was near at hand. I was just discussing with Guillaume what was to be done next, when Orkeke came up to us, and said that a scout had just arrived, and had told him that a white man was camping at a lake some eighteen miles away, and that, for a consideration, he would lend us a couple of horses to take us so far.

In half an hour the horses were driven up; and having made some small presents to Mrs. Orkeke and her family, I hastily left, fearing lest, acting on some new caprice, Orkeke might, at the last moment, find some pretext for taking the horses away from us again.

XV

ON TO SANDY POINT

AT last we said good-bye to the Indians, and set out, accompanied by a man who was to take the horses back, *en route* for a lake called the "Laguna del Finado Romero," after an ill-fated white man, who, like ourselves, had lost his horses in the pampa, and, unluckier than we had been, had failed to fall in with any one on the road, and had finally died of starvation near the lake that now bears his name.

Our horses were lean, overworked, and broken-winded, and we were obliged to ride bare-backed, as the Indians had refused to lend us saddles; but we cared little for such slight drawbacks, in the joy of once more being able to look forward with certainty to a speedy arrival at our destination.

We had only been on foot for three days, but, looking back, it seemed to me an age since I had last bestrode a horse; and the pleasure I experienced, as we broke into a tolerably swift gallop, was heightened by the remembrance of those unpleasant days during which we trudged wearily along on foot, esteeming it a great triumph if we successfully scaled some pigmy hill without having to lie down two or three times to take breath, and when we hardly dared look at the vast expanse of plain before us, lest we should lose courage at the sight. Contrasted with that period of our journey, our present situation was all *couleur de rose*. Our sorry nags seemed gifted with the fleetness of the wind, their distressed puffing sounded in our ears like the proud snorting of the fiery steed scenting the chase, and their irregular pace, half gallop, half stumble, seemed as soft and pleasant as the gentle amble of a pampered park hack.

After about three hours' sharp riding, we reached the lake, beside which was pitched the tent of the white man of whom the Indians had told us. The barking of the dogs warned him of our approach, and he came out to meet us, not a little astonished at our appearance, as the Indians had told him that the Gallegos had risen, and, of course, he had not imagined that any one could have come from Santa Cruz. He kindly welcomed us into his tent, where the first thing that struck my eye, as smacking pleasantly of civilization, was an empty preserved-milk tin. Our new host, whose name was Emilio, was an old acquaintance of Guillaume's, and he very kindly offered to lend us horses to continue our journey to Sandy Point with, as the Indian was returning with those we had come on.

As the weather looked very threatening, and big rain-drops were already beginning to fall, we thought it best to defer our start for another day, feeling that, in one way and another, we had had quite enough wettings lately.

The tent we now found ourselves in seemed "fitted up with all modern conveniences;" indeed, Emilio appeared to be, as he in reality was, rather an amateur than a professional ostrich-hunter, and his neat riding-suit and general clean appearance made me for the first time painfully conscious of the strange scarecrow figure I must have made in the eyes of a civilized human being. The pampa had dealt rather roughly with my wardrobe. I was hatless, shoeless, and coatless, having tossed away or lost all these necessary articles of wear at various periods of my peregrinations. My shirt and trousers were tattered and torn; my hair, which had been a stranger to the comb for weeks, was long and matted; and my face, from continual exposure to sun and wind, had become of a deep Tehuelehe brown. Fortunately, no excuses for my appearance were necessary; and, having dismissed our Indian friend with his horses, we sat down in the tent to discuss some maté and a pipe, over which luxuries Emilio satisfied my voracious appetite for news of the war in the East, with such items of information as he had picked up lately in Sandy Point.

Touching the dinner-hour, which was now approaching, he told us that his companion had gone to the settlement ten days ago to fetch provisions, and as he had not yet come back, he (Emilio) had run short of everything, and had not so much as a biscuit in the place,—a piece of information which gave me a shock, which I trust I bore with more outward composure than my inner feelings warranted. However, when dinner was served, matters turned out to be better than Emilio had represented, and our hearts were gladdened over a puchero of guanaco meat, seasoned with onions, pepper and salt, and other old acquaintances, whose want we had lately so often and so feelingly deplored.

Darkness came on soon after dinner was over, and we were accordingly not long in turning in. All through the night there was a heavy downpour of rain, and as I listened to it pattering on the canvas of our tent, snugly rolled up in my warm capa, I thought, with a shudder, in what a different plight I should have then been had we not had the good fortune to meet the Indians. Instead of lying warm and dry under the shelter of the tent, we should doubtless have been stretched somewhere on the muddy ground, in damp clothes and soaking furs, hungry and sleepless, and exposed to the inclemency of the weather, without even the means of making a fire.

The next day the rain cleared off at about ten o'clock, and Emilio, who was anxious to know what had become of his companion, resolved to accompany us, leaving his tent and horses in charge of a servant. On the previous day I had felt little inconvenience from riding bare-backed, the satisfaction of having a horse at all far outweighing the consideration of any minor discomforts. But to-day I could no longer remain callous to the inconvenience and pain of bumping up and down hour after hour on the back of a not over well-conditioned horse. After the first few miles, the sensation experienced became extremely unpleasant, and gradually developed into a species of mild torture—to culminate, after galloping some thirty miles, in the most excruciating anguish the mind can conceive of. However, we were not to be stopped by mere pain, and jogged along as best we could.

The country we now traversed began to differ essentially from the regions I had hitherto passed through. The monotonous alternation of plains and ravines gave way to a not less monotonous succession of soft swells or undulations. The height of the crests of these undulations was about twenty feet, and the soil which covered them, judging from the appearance of the grass, seemed of a more fertile nature than that of the country further north. As yet, however, there was no appearance of any new species of bush. Occasionally an ostrich would start up at our approach; but already we began to miss the familiar sight of the guanacos, which are, until one arrives as far south as we now were, an inevitable feature of a Patagonian landscape.

After emerging from this undulating tract, the transit of which occupied several hours, we came into an irregularly formed country, abounding in fresh water lakes, which were covered with wild geese and ducks. Here the calafaté bushes seemed to grow stronger and healthier looking, and the now green grass, growing in abundance everywhere, gave an unaccustomed look of fertility to the country. We were not far from Cape San Gregorio, and occasionally we could catch a hazy glimpse of the sea.

Meantime evening came on, and we began to look about for a favourable place to camp at for the night. In casting about we observed a thin column of smoke arising from a small gorge some little way ahead. Thither we accordingly rode, and presently came upon a young fellow who was just making a fire, he having evidently arrived a few minutes ago. His horses were grazing about the cañon. He started up at our approach, and greeted us very cordially, Guillaume being an old acquaintance of his. He turned out to be a Frenchman, and had formerly been cook to the Governor of Sandy Point, but had subsequently taken to ostrich-hunting and trading with the Indians as more congenial pursuits.

He was a very pleasant and lively companion, and we had a very cheerful evening together. Besides, at dinner he gave us some specimens of his art, which stamped him as a master, or at least I thought so then. I actually found a laurel-leaf in the puchero of this epicurean ostrich-hunter, and presently he turned out an *omelette aux fines herbes*, which might have been prepared in a royal kitchen, instead of in the desert, over a smoky, green-wood fire, by the doubtful light of a few stars. As he kindly offered to lend us horses to go on with, there was no necessity for Emilio to accompany us any further, especially as, through our new acquaintance, he had got news of the coming of his absent companion. Before we went to bed, therefore, I thanked him for his kindness, and said good-bye to him, as Guillaume and I intended starting at about three o'clock in the morning, in order to get to Sandy Point the same night. We purposed starting thus early as there was an arm of the sea to cross, which, if we happened to reach it at high water, might detain us for several hours. I also took leave of our host, and then we all went to our beds, to sleep through what I hoped was to be my last night on the pampa.

When the position of the stars seemed to indicate its being about three o'clock, Guillaume and I, after a hasty cup of coffee, bridled the horses that had been lent to us, and waving a silent adieu to our sleeping companions, we rode off through the darkness towards the Cabeza del Mar, or "Head of the Sea," which we hoped to reach at low water. We were not so well mounted as the day before, as we soon discovered to our cost. My horse, in particular, was a lean, raw-boned animal, with a terribly rough gallop, and as the trail had now become swampy and full of holes, it would occasionally stumble and throw me forward in a most punishing manner, and I suffered even more than the day before from the want of a saddle. Meanwhile the darkness slowly gave way to dawn, and by the time the sun had risen, we reined in our panting horses, on whom the steep hills and heavy ground had told severely, at the rocky shores of the Cabeza del Mar. The water was at ebb tide, and we had to wait an hour or two before we could cross over. Cabeza del Mar, marked on the Admiralty charts as Peckett's Harbour, is an inlet of the sea which runs for some distance into the interior.

Having crossed over without any accident, we again continued our journey at a gallop. The ground was very soft, and for miles was half under water. At one spot my horse sank into a quagmire, and it was only with the greatest difficulty that I finally got it out again. Altogether, our horses, which were very thin and in wretched condition, began to show signs of distress, as the hours wore on, and at times we were apprehensive lest they would not be able to reach Sandy Point. Still we splashed on through mire and water, without sparing whip or spur. Now and then we caught sight of the sea, and when the rising wind swept away the mist which obscured the horizon, the snow-clad peaks of the distant Cordilleras showed plainly against the blue sky. We hailed them with delight, for we knew that at the foot of the last spur lay Sandy Point.

Presently we passed a stunted clump of beeches, standing in the midst of the bare plain, like an advanced picket of the dense forests which, a little farther south, clothe the sides of the straits and the broad slopes of the Cordilleras. After having passed so many weeks without having seen any vegetation but the grass and low scrub of the pampas, the sight of these beeches was indescribably refreshing and cheering, and produced the same exhilarating effect on us as the sudden appearance of land after a long sea-voyage does on the traveller, weary of the eternal sameness of sea and sky.

On we went, leaving the beeches behind us, over a broad grass-covered plain, now half under water and a mere swamp, the distant hills growing gradually more and more distinct. By this time I had grown as tired as my horse, and had left off the use of either whip or spur, as it seemed to take no notice of them, just jogging along at its own pace, a kind of slinging shuffle, varied now and then by a lurch forward, as if about to fall,—an ending to our ride which would not have surprised me in the least, considering the condition of the poor animal and the distance we had gone since morning. But the Patagonian horses are wonderfully hardy, and can do an astonishing amount of work, in a condition which makes it seem doubtful whether they will be able to carry their own weight. This was the case with those we were now riding, which were mere skin and bone; and yet we had been already nine hours on the road, scaling steep hills, and staggering over swampy, heavy ground, of the most trying nature.

Time went on. The beeches became more frequent, and finally we arrived at the foot of a thickly wooded hill, which seemed to mark the commencement of a totally new region, for whereas hitherto all vegetation had been scarce and stunted, it now became comparatively varied and luxuriant. Following a beaten track, we rode up the hill through a glade of beeches, which were just bursting into leaf. On reaching its summit I paused, for suddenly flashed on my gaze, lying at the foot of the hill on whose crest I now stood, the shining waters of the Straits of Magellan. With avidity I feasted my eyes, wearied of the eternal monotony of the pampa horizon, on the varied and sunlit scene before me. In strange contrast to the bare plains I had just left was the bold outline of the winding coast, which sank abruptly down, green with dense foliage, to the very edge of the foaming water, whilst in the background rose the gigantic ridges of the Cordilleras, their sharply cut and snow-clad peaks standing plainly defined on the for once cloudless sky.

On the opposite side of the straits the tall cliffs of Terra del Fuego were plainly visible; and presently, emerging from a bend in the coast, a little schooner came skimming down, with all her sails set, and her colours flying, bound, no doubt, for the neighbouring Falkland Islands.

But time was precious, as we wanted to get to Sandy Point before night-time; so off we started again, down the precipitous side of the hill, the bottom of which we reached after many a slip and stumble, the melting of the snows having carried away whole lengths of what had been a beaten path way. The farmhouse of Cabo Negro now came in sight, and near it, grazing at their ease in the fresh young grass, were herds of horses and cattle. As their familiar lowing fell on my ears, my heart quite warmed towards the sleek-coated, gentle-eyed cows, and I bestowed a kindly greeting on them in passing, quite as if they had been human beings. But to me at that moment they represented something more than mere milk and butter in perspective (though that consideration was not altogether absent from my mind). In their staid, respectable demeanour, so different from the wild capers and antics of my late friends, the guanacos, I recognized the softening influences of civilization, and in my present mood I was only too glad to be able to hail its presence under any symbol, even though it were but in the lowly guise of a simple-minded cow.

On reaching the farmhouse, we dismounted for a while, in order to give our horses the rest they sorely needed. The owner, Lieutenant Gallegos, received us very kindly, and asked us into the house to take some refreshment. Whilst the meal was being prepared, I explained to him the circumstances which had brought us into the strange plight in which he beheld us, our saddleless nags and our dilapidated appearance having naturally aroused his curiosity. He was not surprised to hear of the unusually high flood at Gallegos, as, on the melting of the snows, there had been great inundations all round the colony, and an unprecedented snowfall during the winter. The winter itself had been of unusual duration, for although it was now almost summer-time, until a few days since, like ourselves, they had experienced regular wintry weather. In the mean time a repast had been served, and I sat down, actually on a chair, and ate off a plate with knife and fork, feeling quite awkward and bearish, as if I had till then never enjoyed such luxuries. However, this feeling soon wore off, and before I had finished my meal I felt quite at home again. As soon as we had exhausted our respective budgets of news, we said good-bye to Lieutenant Gallegos, and remounted our horses, who had profited by the short respite allowed them, and had become tolerably fresh again.

Our path now lay along the Straits of Magellan. The water almost washed our horses' feet as we rode along the narrow path, for the mainland falls almost vertically down to the water's edge, and is covered with a dense, impenetrable mass of trees and bushes—the latter chiefly of the magnolia species—and one is forced to keep on the meagre strip of stony beach, which in some places is hardly three feet broad. This narrow track was further occasionally obstructed by trunks of beech trees and other drift-wood, torn probably from the land on the opposite side, and swept thither by the sea in its angry moods; and sometimes a still more formidable hindrance would present itself in the shape of a landslip, with a whole slice of virgin forest torn away with it, the trees, bushes, and creepers still green and flourishing. In those cases, where the soil had already been washed away by the sea, all the less durable vegetation having long mouldered away, a prey to the wind and waves, only the dead trees remained, looking sad and ghastly in their untombed nakedness,—some fallen, others still upright, but leaning against each other in forlorn helplessness, their white, bare roots firmly interlaced, and their long, dry arms rattling against each other in the wind, like the bones of so many skeletons.

Following its numerous bends, we rode along the beach for about three hours; and then, in measure as we approached the long sandy strip of land which stretches out into the sea, and which has given the name of Sandy Point to the settlement, the beach got broader, the fall of the land less abrupt, and the forest gradually lightened, till, reaching the Government saw-mill, which is situated at about six miles from the colony, we came to an open plain, studded here and there with beeches, across which we galloped for some time; and finally, having forded one or two small streams, we at last arrived in sight of the town itself.

XVI

MUTINY!

THE colony of Magellan was founded by the Chilian Government in the year 1851. The population of Sandy Point, including the convicts and garrison, and the Swiss settlers of Agna Fresca, numbered, at the time I am speaking of, about eight hundred souls. The town lies at the foot of a high ridge of hills facing the straits. It contained a fort, a church, and some tolerable-looking Government buildings, but, excepting one or two streets in the lower part of the town, the rest of the place had a poor, straggling appearance, the houses being mostly one-storied wooden shanties, and the streets grass-grown and hillocky, with here and there the stump of a beech tree sticking up from the ground. But to me, as I rode through it, just before sundown, tired and fagged with my day's ride, it looked pleasant and cheerful enough, for it held out promises of shelter, rest, and good cheer, after a long, weary time of exposure and hardship, and it was, besides, a connecting link with the outer world, to reach which had been my only thought for weeks,—weeks which, as I looked back on them, in the variety of sensation and incident which had marked their course, seemed almost so many years.

I rode slowly up the main street, letting my eyes wander leisurely over the unaccustomed sights which everywhere met my gaze, and which I greeted inwardly one by one, as it were renewing an old acquaintance. The shops with their many wares displayed in the windows, the knots of drinkers standing at the bars, which in Sandy Point grace every establishment, be it a butcher's or a baker's or a tailor's; the little children playing about the streets; the housewives taking in their little washing from the clothes line, and doing a great deal of gossip over it, as is their wont; the cows coming lowing down from the woods with their calves, and going to their respective homes to be milked; the loungers in collars and neckties (strange sight), who stared at me as I went past,—everything and everybody came in for a share of my attention. Each one sight helped to confirm the complacent feeling of security from further danger which had come over me since I passed the Cabo Negro farm-house. The turn in the long lane had come at last, the chapter of accidents was over, and, like the heroes of the fairy tales, I was to live happy ever after. Alas for human foresight! Could I have foreseen the events which in a few hours were to take place, in all probability I should then and there have turned my horse round and ridden with all speed back to the pampas. But if coming events do cast their shadows before them, it is very seldom that our imperfect mental vision can perceive them, and certainly there was no forecast of the horrors of the coming day in the atmosphere of the settlement of Sandy Point, on the evening of that 10th of November. People came and went, and laughed and talked with each other, just as usual, little thinking that by that time to-morrow they would be flying from their pillaged and burning homes, with their wives and children, and that the colony, now so tranquil and peaceful, would to-morrow be delivered into the hands of a set of sanguinary ruffians, free to indulge in their worst passions unchecked.

There are no inns at Sandy Point, visitors being of rare occurrence, so we put up at the house of an Austrian, named Pedro, who had formerly been an Indian trader, and now kept a small shop. After having indulged in the luxury of a warm bath and a shave, and having made some suitable changes in my raiment, I sat down to dine with Pedro. The havoc I made amongst cheeses, fresh butter, bread, jam, etc., was tremendous. I think—and it is an important consideration which, strange to say, has escaped even Brillat-Savarin—that every man who has any pretensions to considering himself a gastronome, should make it a supreme duty to give his palate a complete rest, at least once a year, and subsist for a month or two on as poor a diet as is compatible with keeping body and soul together. His temporary self-denial will be more than repaid by the renewed sensibility of his palate which will result from such a course, and he will return to his favourite dishes with that fresh zest and exquisite enjoyment which is vouchsafed to most people only in the palmy heyday of their schoolboy appetites.

After dinner I lost no time in going to bed. I had been fifteen hours, not in the saddle, but literally on horseback, and I was weary enough as may be supposed. I felt, as I lay down on my bed, that I had well earned a good night's rest, and was but little prepared for the rude awakening in store for me.

Towards midnight I was aroused by a noise which at first I took for thunder, but which on repetition, to my astonishment, proved to be the report of cannon. While I was still listening and wondering what could be the matter, Guillaume came hurriedly into the room and cried, "The convicts and the soldiers have mutinied, and are firing on the lower town." I was too sleepy to be able to quite seize the situation, and this startling piece of news only elicited a growl from me to the effect that I thought they might have waited till the morning, and I fell back, and was just dozing off again, when a volley of musketry discharged at that moment close to our door, followed by a loud shriek, thoroughly awoke me, and I jumped out of bed and hurriedly put on my clothes.

As soon as all was quiet outside the house, I went to the door and cautiously opened it. It was still dark, but daybreak to all appearance was not far off. The streets near Pedro's house were quite deserted, but in the direction of the plaza there was a great commotion, and the shouting of many voices, the rattling of horses' hoofs over the paved streets, the deep growl of cannon, or the sharp report of a Remington, broke ominously on the silence of the night. Curious to know what was going on, Guillaume and I slipped into the street and stole towards the plaza, in order to question any person we might happen to meet, as to the exact nature of the disturbance. Presently, in running along, I stumbled over something, and on turning back to look I found with a shudder that it was the dead body of a man, probably the one whose shriek we heard a short time ago. We had not gone far, when we saw somebody hastening our way as fast as his legs could carry him. We detained him for a moment, though he was as impatient to be gone as the wedding guest in the ballad, and he told us that the convicts and soldiers had mutinied and had killed the governor of the colony, the captain of the garrison, and all the officers, and were now engaged in fighting among themselves. With this information we went back to the house, wondering what the upshot of the whole affair would be,—a matter which it was rather difficult to foretell, as the Chilian man-of-war generally stationed at Sandy Point was at that time surveying the straits some distance away, and till she arrived the convicts and soldiers would be masters of the situation.

Our evil star, as I remarked to Guillaume, was still in the ascendant; indeed, it was a most peculiar instance of a continued run of bad luck, that *on the very night* of our safe arrival amongst civilized people, after having overcome not a few obstacles which had risen one after the other to frustrate our plans, an event should occur whose ultimate consequences might cause us to regret that we had ever crossed the Gallegos. Besides, it was not as if it were one of the ordinary accidents that may reasonably happen at any moment; far from it, the event in question was of so unusual a nature as to fairly make it improbable that it could happen even once in half a century. This being the case, it was rather provoking that, given all the antecedents of my journey, it should just happen at the very moment of my passing through Sandy Point.

There were as yet, however, no grounds for apprehending anything serious. It was probable that the mutineers, having obtained their liberty, would make use of it to escape as quickly as possible to the pampas, though what they were to do when they got there was best known to themselves. With these and sundry other unpleasant reflections passing through my mind, I lay down on my couch, and went to sleep again. When I awoke it was broad daylight. On opening my eyes, I was startled by the sight of a drunken convict, who was leaning against the door of my room, holding a box of sardines in one hand, and a piece of bread in the other. His Remington rifle, which, judging by the smell of powder it emitted, had been discharged several times, lay on the table beside my bed. He glared stupidly at me as I got up and went past him into the shop, which I found full of convicts and soldiers, who were eating and drinking and squabbling, and brandishing their Remingtons about in such a clumsy way that I expected at any moment to see some accident happen. They told me that they had killed the governor and all his family, and that they were now going off to the pampa to escape to the Argentine Republic. They professed to have no intention of harming any of the colonists, all they required being that they should be allowed to take whatever they wanted, free of payment. They were continually quarrelling among themselves, the chief object of their dispute being the honour, to which every one seemed to lay claim, of having killed the governor,—the truth being that he had not been killed by any one, having escaped on horseback shortly after the revolt broke out. When one crowd left, another would come in, and so on all the morning, till very soon all the drinkables and eatables in Pedro's shop had disappeared.

Most of the mutineers, both soldiers and convicts, were Chilotes, as the people of the island of Chiloe are called. To do them justice, I must say that I have never seen a more repulsively ugly and wretched-looking race than these same Chilotes, at least, if I am to judge of them by the numerous specimens I had the pleasure of seeing at Sandy Point. They are of low stature, and light build, their complexion is swarthy, their foreheads low, and the general expression of their faces is one of brutish stupidity blended with savage ferocity. I think there is, on the whole, very little to choose between them and the Fuegians, who, I believe, are commonly admitted to represent the lowest type of humanity extant.

Meanwhile the day wore on, but the mutineers did not seem in any hurry to quit the colony. It was impossible to leave the house to obtain any news of the revolt, as they were amusing themselves by firing random shots in all directions, during which pastime not a few of their own number were accidentally killed. About this time they commenced a wholesale pillage of the shops, at which task they were assisted by the women and the Chilian colonists generally. I do not think the latter actually took part in any of the acts of violence subsequently committed, but at the commencement of the revolt they certainly fraternized with the mutineers, and in company with the latter, plundered and drank freely. Some colonists who lived opposite Pedro's house were busy all day long in carrying loads of wearing apparel and goods of all descriptions from the various shops into their dwellings. What they were ultimately to do with all their spoils, I suppose they hardly knew themselves, though, if they had not been too drunk, they might have reflected that so soon as order had been restored to the colony, a general search would be made, and they would not only be compelled to disgorge their plunder, but the fact of stolen goods being found in their possession would necessarily implicate them as having taken part in the mutiny. But the whole uprising was marked by the same utter absence of forethought, and the same incomprehensible indifference to inevitable consequences. If any preconcerted plan of action had originally existed, it was certainly not acted upon, and to this fortunate circumstance it is owing that all their intended victims escaped, with the exception of the captain of the garrison.

Towards three o'clock I was agreeably surprised by the sudden appearance of the German steamer in the offing, and I immediately began to make preparations for leaving by her, as I supposed that the mutineers would offer no objection to my taking my departure. My hopes were doomed to be disappointed, however. When the steamer arrived abreast of the English consul's house, which is situated about five miles further up the straits, a little cutter put off from the shore, evidently with the intention of acquainting the people on board the steamer of the mutiny. I watched with anxious eyes to see what the steamer would do. Having parleyed for a while with the people in the cutter, she moved slowly on again towards the colony. Presently the boat of the captain of the port put off from shore and went out to meet her. She had hardly got alongside when a sudden report was heard, and a cannon-ball, fired from the fort, struck the water just under the steamer's bows. It was quickly followed by another, which fell rather wide of the mark. In the mean while the steamer got out of range as quickly as she was able, and keeping well on the opposite side of the straits, she soon passed the colony, and gradually disappeared from sight, taking the boat of the captain of the port with her.

It appeared that the latter had been manned by several mutineers, who, disregarding the maxim anent honour among thieves, had made off with their own and their companions' share of certain moneys which had been plundered from the military chest. They had hoped to palm themselves off on the authorities on board as peaceful citizens, who had made good their escape from the dangers of the revolt, but the captain took the liberty of doubting their representations, and put them all into irons. They were eventually brought back to Sandy Point by an American man-of-war, which met the German steamer a few days afterwards.

Partly from rage at having been duped by their comrades, and partly from pure love of mischief, the mutineers had endeavoured to shell the steamer, and their first shot was very nearly attended with disastrous success.

I consoled myself for the disappointment I had just experienced, by the thought that the Pacific steamer for Monte Video, the *Cotopaxi* was due on the following day, and I was determined that I would not miss her in the same way. There was no other steamer after her for another fortnight, and it would indeed be a fatality if, after all the efforts I had made in order to reach Sandy Point in time to take her, she should actually pass by before my very eyes, without my being able to go on board.

As it was possible that she might arrive at any moment, I resolved to go immediately to the English consul's house, in order to go on board with him, for I did not doubt that he would put off to warn her not to approach the colony.

Without losing any time, therefore, I started off with Guillaume. On the way we met several bands of mutineers, who were in a very advanced state of intoxication. They told us that they were going to set fire to the town, and leave that night for the pampas, but though they were always threatening to shoot one another, they did not molest us in any way. I noticed that they were all dressed in new clothes, and some even had as many as three waistcoats on.

When I arrived at the English consul's house, I found there was no one in it except the foreman of the saw-mill, a Scotchman, who had but recently arrived at the colony, and who was by no means tranquil in his mind as to the turn events had taken. He told me that Mr. Dunsmuir, the consul, had gone off in his cutter to meet the German steamer, but that he had not yet returned, probably owing to a strong head wind which was then blowing. I remained, therefore, to await his coming, and Guillaume went back to the colony, to see how matters were going.

XVII

FLIGHT TO THE WOODS

I FOUND McGregor, my new companion, in a state of despondent dread lest a party of mutineers should arrive from Sandy Point "and murder us a'." I endeavoured to convince him that there was no danger, as indeed I believed there was not, but he refused to be comforted, and grew so gloomy at the thought of the terrible fate in store for him, that at last I gravely said, "Well, I see there is no use in hiding the truth from you. We are in a most dangerous plight, and if bad fortune does lead the soldiers here, we are as likely as not to get our throats cut." This lugubrious intimation had the effect I anticipated. Feeling that nature unaided was not strong enough to sustain him under the present critical circumstances, McGregor applied himself so assiduously to a jar of whisky that was fortunately at hand, that in a very short time he became quite cheerful, and even warlike, and sang "Scots wha ha'e wi' Wallace bled" with astonishing vigour and persistency, till, yielding to the soft influences of his native stimulant, he at last sank into that sweet, calm slumber, from which the awakening is "hot coppers."

Meanwhile evening came on apace, but no signs of the consul, and I began to fear that he had been blown too far out to sea to get back again that night. To pass away the time, I inspected the house, which was one-storied, and consisted of two large front rooms, a sitting-room, and a bedroom, behind which were two smaller compartments, one used as a larder, and the other as a kitchen. From the back door one had only to step out to find one's self in a dense beech forest.

Just as it was getting dark, I heard the sound of horses' hoofs, and Guillaume galloped up to the house, breathless and excited. He told me that matters had taken a very serious turn in the colony; the mutineers had committed several acts of violence and a general massacre being apprehended, great numbers of the colonists were flying to the woods. He himself had had a very narrow escape. He had been seized by a party of mutineers, who were making preparations for leaving for the pampas and who wished to requisition his services as guide to Santa Cruz. All his remonstrances were in vain, and they plainly intimated to him that he had to choose between accompanying them and having a bullet put through him; he was compelled, therefore, to appear to assent. In order to gain time he asked that he might be allowed to go to Pedro's house to fetch some clothes, and his request being granted, two soldiers were sent with him to prevent any attempt he should make to escape. They were fortunately so drunk, however, that they had hardly been a few minutes in the house when they lay down and soon fell fast asleep. Profiting by this lucky circumstance, Guillaume lost no time in jumping on a horse which happened to stand in Pedro's yard and in a few seconds he placed himself out of danger of pursuit.

All this news was the reverse of reassuring, and I began to think that McGregor's fears were, after all, not wholly unfounded. The consul's house was only a few yards off the road which led from Sandy Point to the Swiss colony at Agna Fresca, and at any time we might expect an unpleasant visit from some of the soldiers, who were continually going that way in search of horses or plunder. To make matters worse, neither Guillaume nor I had a revolver, and although we searched all over the house, we could not find an arm of any description. If attacked, therefore, we had no means of defending ourselves,—a consideration which did not tend to allay our apprehensions.

After supper, we made preparations for passing the night. McGregor, who in the mean time had awakened, made up a bed for himself on the floor; and although I advised him not to, he would insist on taking off his clothes. I lay down on a sofa, to take a short nap, pending the consul's arrival, which I hoped would not now be long delayed. I soon fell asleep, but at about midnight I awoke, roused by the pattering of rain on the roof. I got up and looked out at the weather. The night was pitch dark, and the rain was falling in torrents; there was a stormy wind blowing, and I could plainly hear the hoarse roar of the waves on the beach. I went back to the sofa, but lay tossing about for a long time, unable, tired as I was, to go to sleep again.

An hour went by, and I was just dozing off, when I thought I heard a slight tap at the door. Hurriedly lighting the lamp, I got up and looked out. Something touched my hand, and looking down I saw a little boy standing close to me. His first words were—

"My mamma is waiting at the bottom of the garden, and wants to know whether she may come in?"

"Certainly, my boy," I said; "but who is your mother?"

"My father is the governor and we have had to run away from the town, for the soldiers are burning the houses and killing everybody."

With that he ran away into the rain and the darkness, and came back after a second or two, followed by a lady, with several children and two maid-servants.

I immediately took them into the bedroom, and handed an armchair to Mrs. D——, the governor's wife, who was pale with exhaustion and suffering, and almost in a fainting condition. As soon as she was sufficiently rested to be able to speak, she told me that on the previous night, shortly after twelve o'clock, she had been startled from her sleep by the discharge of cannon, with which the mutineers had signalized the commencement of the revolt. Her husband immediately rushed into the street. He had hardly been gone two minutes, when suddenly a hail of mitrailleuse bullets began to crash through the house, riddling the very walls of her bedroom. By a miracle, in the midst of this deadly fire, she had time to collect all her children, and escape with them unhurt into the street by a back door. In a few seconds more the house was in flames, and as she hurried away, she could hear the jubilant shouts with which the mutineers greeted the supposed successful slaughter of her husband and his family. She managed to escape to a little house on the beach, where she had remained hidden during the day without having been detected. But towards night, the uproar and fighting amongst the mutineers increased, several houses were set fire to, and fearing that any moment a passing soldier might burst into the house and discover her, as soon as it got dark she had decided on attempting to reach the English consul's house. By chance she had learned during the daytime that her husband had escaped, and that in all probability he had gone to fetch the Chilian man-of-war *Magellanes,* now at Skyring Water, to put down the revolt.

I told her that Mr. Dunsmuir would in all probability not be back that night, but that in the mean time I should be glad to render her any assistance that she might require.

The children, the eldest of whom was the little boy who had come to the door first, and he was only seven, were dressed in whatever clothes the servants had hurriedly been able to snatch up on the night of the first alarm.

The poor things were in a terrible plight. They had been more than two hours on the road from Sandy Point, and were drenched to the skin with the rain and mire. They had eaten nothing for twenty-four hours. I took them in some tea; but rest being what they chiefly required, with the help of mattresses and rugs, etc., we managed to make some tolerably comfortable beds for them. Having done this, we withdrew to the sitting-room, there to consult as to our plan of action, should the mutineers come to the house.

In the midst of our discussion, there was another knock, and on the door being opened, two more fugitives from the colony, an Irishman and his wife, made their appearance. Both seemed to have had recourse to strong stimulants to support their courage, and under the circumstances they were certainly not a desirable addition to our party.

During all this time McGregor had preserved a cheerful, unconcerned demeanour. He had been particularly active in his attentions to the D—— family, to the extent of insisting, with well-meant but misplaced zeal, that all should swallow a drop of whisky before going to bed. He found the new comers did not require so much pressing.

Guillaume and I were sitting by the fire in the kitchen, trying to get a little sleep, of which we were sorely in need, when suddenly there was a loud banging at the front door, followed by a loud chorus of oaths and vociferation. We immediately ran into the sitting-room, and Guillaume went to open the door, whilst I took the lamp into the kitchen. I had hardly put it down, when I heard a crash in the front room, the house was filled with shrieks, and the Irish couple, McGregor and, as I thought, Guillaume, rushed madly past me into the forest. Seized with the panic, I followed them for a moment; but reflection returning, I went back to the house, ashamed of my want of courage. I found half a dozen drunken soldiers in the sitting-room, parleying with Guillaume. Owing to the darkness, they had fortunately not discovered the other room, where Mrs. D—— was concealed; and in order to divert their attention from it, we induced them to go into the kitchen. There we plied them with more whisky, in the hopes of quickly reducing them to a state of complete inebriety. The transition phase was not a very pleasant one, inasmuch as they never let go their carbines, and frequently, half in joke, half in earnest, they pointed them threateningly at us. At times, too, they would wander into the sitting-room and then moments of terrible suspense ensued for us, lest they should open the door of the bedroom. We were careful always to follow them, and had made up our minds, in the event of their attempting anything of the kind, to suddenly throw ourselves upon the two men nearest us, seize their carbines, which were sixteen-repeating Winchesters, and open fire on the lot. There was every chance in favour of the success of such a measure, as the mutineers were already so drunk that they could hardly stand, and if taken by surprise would have been too bewildered to offer any resistance.

The tension of these moments was heightened by the probability that at any moment Mrs. D——'s babies might begin to cry, and thus reveal the secret of the room. Miraculously enough, however, they kept quiet, and we always managed to get the men back to the kitchen without the dreaded crisis occurring. It seemed as if they never would leave. Twenty times they got to the front door, and we began to breathe afresh, thinking they were at last off, but twenty times, for some reason or other, they would come back again. From their conversation it was very hard to find out what they exactly wanted. Those who were still sufficiently sober to speak articulately, at times told us that they were going to start off to the pampa immediately, and at others that they intended holding the colony against all comers. At one moment they would be maudlinly affectionate; at another, they would lengthily discuss which mode of killing us was preferable,—shooting us or cutting our throats. Of course, we were always on the alert, and ready to make good our objections to either of these methods.

At last we had the indescribable satisfaction of seeing them depart for good. Guillaume followed them at some distance, to give the alarm in case they should come back, whilst I ran to the bedroom to tell Mrs. D—— that for the moment the danger was over. What she must have suffered all this time may be imagined. For two hours, every second of which must have seemed an eternity to her, she had been expecting to see the door burst open at any moment, and herself and her children at the mercy of the mutineers, of whose murderous intentions towards her she had had terrible proof in the bombarding of her house on the night of the commencement of the revolt. But her courage had not given way, as it might well have done under even less trying circumstances and I found her, though pale and prostrate, thoroughly calm and collected. I hurriedly told her that at any moment the mutineers might come back, and that we had better leave the house, and fly to the woods.

We accordingly set out immediately. I took two of the smaller children in my arms, the maids each carried one, and the others walked by the side of their mother; and Guillaume, who had returned after having seen the soldiers safely off to the bottom of the garden, brought up the rear, carrying a mattress and some rugs and blankets. We then dived into the forest. It was still raining, and the night was as dark as could be. At every step we would meet with some mishap, now stumbling over the fallen trunk of a tree, and now slipping into some boggy hole. The children, who had hitherto behaved admirably, having borne hunger and cold and fatigue without a murmur, could now hardly be kept from crying. I carried a little girl of about four years old; her shoes and stockings had been lost in the hurry of collecting the rugs and bedclothes, and her uncovered feet were icily cold. But though I could hear her sob now and then on my shoulder, she was too brave to cry aloud. How the two babies lived through all this exposure was a miracle.

After having walked for about half an hour, for we could make but slow progress, we came to a spot which seemed far enough from the house to be safe, and there we spread out the two mattresses on the wet ground, under the lea of the trunk of a fallen beech tree. The whole party managed to lay down on this rough bed, and, having covered them over with the rugs and blankets Guillaume had brought, we left them, to go back to the house to fetch some provisions and some more coverings, for there was no knowing how many days we might be compelled to pass in the woods.

We went very cautiously towards the house, as we could hear voices in the kitchen, and feared lest the soldiers might have returned already. The strains of "Scots wha ha'e," which pleasantly smote on our ears, reassured us, however, and we went boldly forward. We found that the Irish couple and McGregor had returned; they were toasting their happy escape with more whisky. McGregor was delighted to see that we were still alive, and said he had ran away at the approach of the soldiers, because, "I dinna speak Spanish, ye ken."

We were cold and exhausted with the night's exertions, so whilst Guillaume went to see whether the coast was clear, McGregor set about making coffee, and I busied myself collecting provisions and other necessaries for taking with us to the woods.

Guillaume soon came back, bringing three carbines, which he had found at the bottom of the garden. From the marks in the ground, he surmised that, under the influence of their deep potations, the soldiers had probably lain down to sleep there, and on awakening, had forgotten their arms. This was indeed a prize. Each carbine still contained some six or seven charges. As McGregor would have nothing to do with a weapon, Guillaume and I kept one each, and hid the other away in a bush near the house. As good luck, like bad, seldom comes singly, whilst rummaging about the bedroom in search of the little girl's stockings, I found a revolver. This might prove a more valuable weapon under certain circumstances than the carbine even, and with it safe in my coat pocket, I felt quite a different man.

We were just pouring out the coffee, having made all preparations for finally leaving the house, when Guillaume, who was always on the look-out, rushed suddenly in, and shouting "Run for your lives!" seized me by the arm, and dragged me out of the house. We had just time to snatch up the carbines and dash into the woods, when we heard the soldiers banging at the front door. We did not stop till we had got some distance into the forest. Guillaume told me that there were about a dozen soldiers, amongst whom, doubtless, the three whose carbines he had taken. What they would do on not finding them anywhere in the house, we did not know, but it was not impossible that in their rage they might set fire to the house, and perhaps follow us into the woods. We now deeply regretted having tarried so long in the house, as we had now no provisions to take back to our charges. Whilst debating what to do, we were startled by the sharp crack of a rifle, discharged close to us, followed by the sound of approaching voices; and fearing the soldiers were in pursuit of us, we hurried as fast as possible to where we had left Mrs. D——.

On reaching the spot, we found she had risen, anxious on account of our long absence, and startled by the shot she had just heard. Without saying that I thought we were being followed, I told her that it was perhaps better that we should go still further into the forest, and without losing a second we gathered up the children, and again commenced our pilgrimage, plunging deeper and deeper into the dense mass of underwood, till we had got so far that pursuit seemed impossible.

By this time all the younger children were crying bitterly for want of food. A tin of preserved milk, which I had put in my pocket, had dropped out somehow, and it now became almost a matter of life and death that the babes should have some nourishment. Feeling the urgency of the case, Guillaume and I again started towards the house, hoping that the soldiers had given up their search for us, and had perhaps gone back to Sandy Point. We crept along with beating hearts, starting at the crackling of the branches under our feet, and fearing to find a foe concealed behind every tree, till we at last got to the open near the house. Under cover of some bushes, we crept close up to it. By the hum of voices we could tell that the soldiers were still inside, and presently one came out of the house and stood peering into the wood for a short time, standing so close to us that we could hear his breathing. After he had gone inside, we profited by the opportunity to slip back into the wood, and having made a circuit, we ensconced ourselves on an eminence on the other side of the house, where we were more secure, and where we could better watch the coming and going of our enemies.

There we lay, hour after hour, and still they did not leave,—they were in warm quarters, and the whisky was doubtless too strong an attraction for them. What, I began to think, if they should not leave all day? Our only chance would be to steal into the house after dark, and risk the rest. But it was doubtful whether the younger children could live till then without some nourishment. The tin of milk I had lost would have saved all anxiety, and I half made up my mind to start off and follow the path I had taken from the house to the woods, on the desperate chance of perhaps finding it again. Fortunately matters did not reach that pitch, for at last, after having impatiently waited for about three hours, we saw ten or twelve soldiers leave the house, mount their horses, and ride off in the direction of Sandy Point. We immediately quitted our watch-tower, and ran as fast as we could towards the house; but to our horror, just as we got to the door, we heard voices within again. We were desperate by this time; besides, it was too late to turn back, so, holding our guns in readiness, we cautiously approached the doorway. Then an anticlimax; for suddenly the Irishwoman, followed by her spouse, rushed out and almost received our fire.

On hearing Guillaume's shout of warning, they had waited a moment too long and before they could get out of the place the soldiers were upon them. They had furiously demanded the missing carbines, but of course they were not to be found anywhere, whereupon they threatened to burn the house down. Here again the whisky saved the situation. They lingered so long over the cask that they quite forgot to look for the carbines, much less to go off in pursuit of us. Two or three of them went a few yards into the wood, and fired off a single shot at random, but they probably thought it would be dangerous to risk themselves too far, and they accordingly went back to their comrades. They stayed as long as the whisky lasted, and then went off again.

We lost no time in collecting a quantity of provisions, tins of preserved meats and soups, milk, ham, eggs, etc., etc., to which I added some plates, saucepans, knives, spoons, in fact, everything necessary for a prolonged sojourn in the woods. I told McGregor to come with us, if he liked, as to all appearance the mutineers seemed in no hurry to leave for the pampas, and sooner or later he might get into trouble. The Irish couple, having found a case of sherry, seemed to think their lines cast in a very pleasant place, and as the soldiers had as yet not done them any grievous harm, they made up their minds to stay.

Loaded with the remaining blankets and with the provisions, we made our way back as quickly as possible to Mrs. D—— who, as we had been away for more than four hours, had become quite alarmed lest some mishap had befallen us. We turned out the provisions, soon made a fire, and having dissolved some milk for the younger children, we commenced to prepare a substantial meal, of which every one stood in great need. We were just beginning to feel a little more at our ease, the children had been able to dry their clothes and warm themselves by the fire, some meat we had set to roast was nearly done to a turn, and, feeling secure now from all danger, we were able for the first time to quietly talk of the late events a discuss the probability of the speedy arrival of the Chilian man-of-war,—when two women came running through the woods towards us, pale and frightened, calling out as they got near, "The soldiers, the soldiers! Run for your lives!"

We all started to our feet in dismay. It was perhaps already too late to fly. We were at all events armed, and could at least make a good stand if necessary. Meanwhile we hurriedly lifted the children in our arms, and leaving everything else behind us, we again "moved on," turning our heads at every second, to be prepared should the soldiers arrive. No one appeared, however, and it seemed merely a false scare of the women. The forest had become so dense that occasionally we had to pick our way through thick underwood. The ground was a mere swamp, full of treacherous holes, and the rain and moisture clinging to the leaves of the bushes drenched us all to the skin as we brushed through them. But still we kept on, determined to place such a distance between the road and our camp as to leave us perfectly at ease as regards the mutineers, who would certainly never take the trouble of looking so far into the wood for anybody, even if they were to stop another month round the colony.

When we reached a small open in the thicket, where the ground was tolerably dry, we set down the children, and returned on our tracks to fetch the mattresses, coverings, and food we had left behind. We found everything just as we had left it, and not a sign of any one having been near the place. The women who had run past us had, perhaps, heard some branches crackle, and had immediately concluded that the mutineers were coming. However, there was nothing to be done but to carry everything to our new camping-place,—no easy task, as both Guillaume and myself were completely done up with our continued exertions, and the mattresses and various other articles were in themselves heavy enough.

We had hidden our charges so well that we could not find them ourselves and only after a great deal of searching, quite by accident, we happened to stumble on the place again. To keep off the wet, which was dropping from the trees, we rigged up a kind of tent over the mattresses with some blankets, and under its shelter the whole party lay huddled together. We then tried to make a fire, but as the wood was wet it could not be got to burn, and only blinded us with smoke. After a great deal of blowing, we at last succeeded in raising a fair glow, by the aid of which we managed to cook a meal, which was actually eaten. And quite time it was, too, as the children had had nothing but the milk for nearly forty-eight hours.

It was now about four o'clock. I became anxious to know what was going on in the colony, and whether there was any possibility of the mutineers leaving soon. Leaving McGregor in charge of the camp, Guillaume and I made our way down to the road, and keeping under cover of the wood, slowly proceeded in the direction of the colony, in the hopes of meeting some one who could give us some news. We had not gone very far when we saw a stout little man coming running along the road at full speed. Guillaume recognized him as one of the bakers of Sandy Point, and called to him to stop, as he ran past us. As soon as he could find breath to speak, he said that a short time before the house where he lived had been attacked by the soldiers, two of his companions had been killed, and he had only saved himself by jumping out of a window, just as the mutineers were standing in the doorway of his room, with fixed bayonets, inviting him to pass through their midst. There was hardly any one left in the colony, most of the inhabitants having taken refuge in the woods. He had seen several dead bodies lying about as he had hurried away, but having never been out of his house since the commencement of the revolt, he could give us little information as to the doings of the mutineers.

We went back to the consul's house with him. The Irishwoman was still there, and was sleeping peacefully in an armchair; her husband we found lying in the kitchen, with several severe head-wounds. A pillaging party had evidently gone through the place, for drawers were upset, crockery smashed, curtains torn down, and general disorder prevalent everywhere. The baker was in a hurry to be off to the woods, for after his recent narrow escape he had a wholesome, but perhaps excessive, dread of being suddenly seized by the mutineers again.

But though we had plenty of provisions of all kinds, there was neither bread nor biscuit in the house, so I asked him,—flour, eggs, and butter being at hand,—to make the dough for some cakes, which could be baked up in the woods at our leisure. Very reluctantly he agreed to do so, on condition that Guillaume should watch the road, to give timely warning of the approach of danger. Presently Guillaume called me, and on going out I saw a dense cloud of smoke rising in the direction of the colony. The convicts had evidently set fire to the town, a prelude, perhaps, to their departure. There was no wind, and soon a heavy downpour of rain commenced; but we had little hope that a stick would be left standing in the whole settlement, which was built exclusively of timber. The dough being ready, though I think it had not been kneaded very carefully, we went back into the wood, losing our way as on the former occasion, and had it not been for the familiar strains of "Scots wha ha'e!" with which McGregor was cheering the children, and which at last guided us to the camp, we might have wandered about for hours.

We were now quite a large party, the possibility of being again disturbed by the mutineers was out of the question, and if only we had been able to make a good blazing fire, than which there is nothing so cheering to the spirits, we might, comparatively speaking, have felt fairly comfortable. But whatever wood we could collect was quite wet, and it was difficult to get it to burn sufficiently to cook the dinner by.

Under shelter of the improvised tent we had managed to rig up, and with the aid of the few coverings procured from the consul's house, Mrs. D—— and the children were fortunately kept tolerably dry and warm, and, overcome with the anxieties and exertions of the day, they were able to forget their troubles in sleep. As for myself and the other men, we tried for some time to do likewise, but having no coverings, the cold and wet effectually kept us awake, and we passed the night huddled round the smouldering logs, listening to the monotonous pattering of the rain on the canopy of leaves above us, and longing wearily for the morning.

It broke at last, and with it came better weather. As soon as the sun was well up, I went down to the house to see if there was anything new. On reaching a point from which the settlement was visible, from the changed aspect of the town it was evident that the fire had done great ravages. It was, however, too far off for me to recognize whether many of the houses were left standing, which, considering the nature of their construction, was not probable. A thin column of smoke was still rising from one part, but the fire itself seemed spent. I then looked down the straits towards Dawson's Island, but as yet there was no sign of any coming steamer. The Pacific steamer *Cotopaxi* was due on the day before, and as it is very unusual for the vessels of that line to be behind time, I concluded that she had been met by the English consul, and was possibly awaiting the arrival of the Chilian man-of-war, whose coming could not now be long delayed, before approaching the colony.

On my way back to our forest sanctuary, I stumbled on a knot of Chilian women, who told me they had escaped from the colony the previous night, for fear of being taken to the pampas by the mutineers, who were making preparations for leaving immediately. They all had big bundles of clothes with them, and, strange to say, all wore brand-new shawls and gowns. I had not the slightest doubt but that they had done their share in the general plundering. It was good news, at all events, to hear that the mutineers were at last really off, of which the burning of the colony was the best proof.

After breakfast I started off with Guillaume, with the intention of going to Sandy Point, if possible, and discovering the real state of affairs there. But on reaching the road just below the consul's house, to our surprise we found it thronged with fugitives from the settlement, who were issuing from all parts of the woods, where they had been hiding. On looking seawards the reason became apparent. Steaming along at full speed, and already nearly opposite the house, we saw the long-expected *Magellanes*, the Chilian man-of-war. I immediately ran back to take the welcome news to Mrs. D——, that her troubles were now over. For the last time we carried the children through the wood down to Mr. Dunsmuir's house, which, by the time we got there, was crowded with women and children, carrying such of their household goods as they had been able to take with them in their flight.

As soon as the *Magellanes* arrived in front of the house, a boat was sent off to the shore, in which Mrs. D—— and her children embarked to meet her husband, who was safe on board. Shortly after, another larger boat came to fetch off the other women and children.

Here a rather ludicrous scene ensued. Just before the boat touched land, the people on shore were suddenly seized with panic, at the sight of some dark bodies advancing on the road from Sandy Point, and which they thought were the soldiers coming towards them. Immediately the air was filled with shrieks, and, throwing down their bundles, they all rushed into the water to meet the advancing boat. The sailors had to keep them off with their oars, or they would have swamped the boat. Meanwhile the foe came nearer, the shrieks grew louder, some of the men even sharing in the general weakness, till at last the coming squadron of horsemen resolved itself into a herd of cows, who came trotting leisurely down the road, ignorant of the panic their presence had created.

The women and those of the men who chose to go were at last brought safely on board, and the *Magellanes* steamed slowly up the straits towards the colony. Guillaume and I had already started off some time before, and we arrived at the first house in the settlement almost as soon as she arrived abreast of the pier.

XVIII

RESCUE AND DEPARTURE

AS we got nearer to the town it became evident that the better portion had been burned down; of the fort, the hospital, the Government buildings, and a great many private houses, nothing remained but a smoking heap of charred timbers. The first house I entered was Pedro's,—the one in which I had slept on the night of my arrival. The state of things inside was deplorable; the shop had been completely ransacked of its contents; the taps of the casks had been turned on, and the wine and aguadiente had run out on the floor, which was strewn with the *debris* of crockery and glassware, broken bottles, half-emptied tins of preserved meats, odd boots, wearing apparel, rice and flour,—the remains, in fact, of what had once constituted Pedro's stock-in-trade. The other rooms bore marks of the same spirit of wanton destruction. Everything smashable had been smashed, and everything conveniently portable had been carried off. The pillaging had been done with remarkable thoroughness—no article seemed to have been too insignificant to escape the rapacity of the marauders, who had thought it worth while to take the cruet-stand, the clock, and the knives and forks of ordinary household use even.

Opposite Pedro's was the baker's house, which had been stormed by the mutineers, the owner having unwisely closed his doors and refused them admission. They killed two of its inmates, and the others had a narrow escape from sharing the same fate, just managing to take flight unhurt under a shower of bullets. Walking down to the plaza, I passed several dead bodies, chiefly of convicts or soldiers. The streets were as yet almost completely deserted, but on turning a corner I found myself face to face with a villainous-looking man, who, on seeing me, suddenly pointed his gun at me, and for a second I thought he was going to fire. He lowered his weapon immediately, however, saying that he had taken me for a mutineer!

I had not the slightest doubt that he was one. In fact, not a few of those who took a very active part in the mutiny remained behind in Sandy Point, when their companions left for the pampas, either because they were too drunk to be able to follow them, or because they calculated on being able to pass themselves off on the authorities as peaceful and inoffensive citizens, and thus escape the punishment they had so well deserved. Hence the officious zeal with which this man had felt himself called upon to offer to shoot me, in the hopes of impressing me with his profound sympathies for the cause of order.

In the mean time some forces were landed from the *Magellanes*, and gradually the colonists began to flock down to the town from all parts of the woods, or from wherever they had been hiding during the revolt. Many came back to find their houses burned to the ground; and there were few who were not completely ruined by the wholesale and wanton destruction of their property.

It was estimated that damage to the amount of about $500,000 had been done,—a very large sum indeed, considering the size of the town and the calling of its inhabitants. About sixty persons perished during the revolt, and several died subsequently from the effects of their wounds. Strange to say, the day after the mutineers left Sandy Point, no less than three men-of-war lay anchored in the straits in front of the town. Amongst them was a United States' steamer, which had been warned by the German packet of the mutiny, and which, but for the heavy weather encountered off Cape Virgines, might have arrived at the colony on Tuesday morning, and have quelled the revolt before it had developed its worst features.

The mutineers had chosen a favourable moment for their rising. Most of the colonists were away seal-fishing, and the man-of-war generally stationed in the straits was temporarily absent from Sandy Point, being engaged on a survey of Skyring Water. The nominal head of the mutineers was a sergeant of the name of Riquelmes. Their plan had originally been to kill the governor and any of the Government officials obnoxious to them, and then immediately set out for the pampas, and cross the Santa Cruz River into Argentine territory, where these naïve scoundrels imagined they would be hailed as an acquisition, and be received with open arms by the authorities. On a par with such absurd reasoning was their conduct throughout the revolt, and when they left Sandy Point they loaded their pack-horses with bales of shawls, dresses, ponchos, and similar useless articles, but with not an ounce of provisions of any kind.

Riquelmes, as I have said, was their nominal chief, but he dared not, had he wished to, enforce his authority, and each mutineer plundered or murdered at his own sweet will, without reference to the doings of his comrades. Owing to this absence of organization, their intended victims, with the exception of the captain of the garrison, were fortunately able to escape. The governor, Major D————, on hearing the first alarm, had run into the streets. A passing soldier, without recognizing him, struck him over the head with a gun, and he fell senseless. When he recovered, aided by the darkness he managed to reach a house on the outskirts of the town, where he was well received and enabled to dress his wound. He then procured a horse, and after an unbroken ride of twenty-three hours, arrived at Skyring Water just in time to catch the *Megellanes*, which was getting up steam preparatory to leaving, and apprise the captain of the mutiny. The captain of the garrison, less fortunate, was murdered as he was leaving his bedroom, and his dead body was barbarously mutilated before the eyes of his wife and children. The other officials escaped.

During the two ensuing days the mutineers were chiefly occupied in drinking and plundering,—pastimes which they varied with occasional fights among themselves. On the first day they had respected the lives and persons of the colonists, and many of the latter, foreseeing that this moderation might not be of long duration, wisely withdrew from the town and hid themselves in the woods, with their wives and children. Those who remained behind, in the hopes of being able to save their homes and property from destruction, soon had cause to regret their imprudence. The conduct of the mutineers, in measure as the effects of the continued drinking in which they indulged began to tell upon them, grew more and more violent, and before long, breaking all bounds, they gave themselves up to the most ferocious licence. It is not necessary to recount the details of the horrible scenes that took place; as may be imagined, given the antecedents of these men, human life was of as little account with them as female honour. Though there was nothing to be gained by it, they seemed to find a peculiar satisfaction in destroying everything that was destructible, and it was not from any want of intention that the whole colony was not burned to the ground by them, but simply that they were too intoxicated to be able to carry out the necessary arrangements for so doing with sufficient thoroughness.

In the midst of their orgies they were surprised by the appearance of the *Magellanes* early on Wednesday morning. Thereupon they hurriedly collected some forty horses, which they loaded with all kinds of plunder, but forgetting, as I have already said, incredible though it may seem, to take any provisions with them; and the whole crowd, which numbered about 180 souls, including some women, then started off for Cabo Negro on foot. At that place they expected to find sufficient horses to mount everybody, as most of the horses belonging to the colonists were kept there, on account of there being little or no pasturage in the vicinity of Sandy Point In this expectation, however, they were disappointed,—the farm-owner had taken the precaution of driving the whole of his stock out of harm's way, and the mutineers, on arriving at Cabo Negro, found themselves obliged to abandon the useless plunder they had brought from the colony, for most of them were already tired out, and required the few horses they possessed for more practical purposes than that of carrying bales of guanaco mantles and dry goods. As many as three men had to ride on each horse, and even then a great number had to drag themselves along on foot as best they might. The whole band, therefore, moved very slowly, and they were, moreover, under continual dread of the arrival of a pursuing party from the colony.

For some reason known only to those having authority, no such party was despatched, however; though there is little doubt that forty or fifty men, well armed and well mounted, might easily have brought the mutineers to bay, and effected their capture without much trouble. Many had already thrown their guns and ammunition away, and now that they were brought face to face with almost certain starvation, would have been glad to surrender on any terms.

In the evening, though they could ill spare them, they had to kill two or three horses for food. The next day they fell in with an ostrich-hunter, who, not knowing what had taken place during his absence, was quietly returning to Sandy Point. His troop of horses was, of course, an invaluable prize to the mutineers, and him they forced to go with them, in order that with his dogs he might help to supply them with food. He contrived to lag behind the main band, however, and when once fairly amongst the foot stragglers, he suddenly turned round, and, galloping away, made good his escape, unpursued by the mutineers, who had no inclination to tire their horses unnecessarily.

They now conceived the plan of surprising the Indians, with the object of massacring them and seizing their horses and dogs, but unforeseen circumstances again conspired to frustrate their intentions. Five or six mutineers had left Sandy Point on the first day of the mutiny, and these men, on passing through the Indian encampment, besides stealing several horses, had killed an Indian who had remonstrated with them. This incident put the Indians on the alert; they despatched scouts in all directions, and as soon as these latter announced the coming of the main band, the camp was hurriedly broken up, and long before the mutineers arrived at Campo de Batalla, the site of the encampment, the Indians were half way to the Cordilleras, and far out of reach of pursuit.

The day after their last disappointment poor Isidoro fell into their hands. He had crossed the Gallegos, which in the mean time had fallen considerably, two days before, and was travelling leisurely towards Sandy Point, little dreaming of what was in store for him, when one evening, on turning a bend in some cañon, he suddenly stumbled on the mutineers' camp. He was immediately surrounded, dragged from his horse, and taken to Riquelmes, who, without saying why or wherefore, ordered him to prepare to be shot within five minutes. Any attempt at resistance was, of course, useless, and Isidoro quietly resigned himself to his fate. Ten men were told off to do the fatal office, and Riquelmes was just going to give the command to fire, when it suddenly occurred to him that Isidoro might be useful for tracking the Indians, to find whom the mutineers still thought it was possible, and accordingly he agreed to spare Isidoro's life, warning him that should he attempt to escape he would be punished with immediate death.

The next day they continued their march. Isidoro, surrounded by a strong guard, was allowed to ride on horseback, his other horses, twenty-seven in number, being of course requisitioned by the mutineers. During the first day no opportunity to escape presented itself, but on the second day such an occasion occurred, and Isidoro adroitly profited by it. In the course of the march some specks were observed moving about on the horizon, which Riquelmes and his followers fancied must be the Indians; and appeal being made to Isidoro, he confirmed their supposition, although his own superior power of vision enabled him to detect that the specks in question were nothing but guanacos. Whereupon ensued great excitement. A halt was immediately made, and a council of war held, with the object of determining some ruse by means of which to obtain the Indians' horses. After everybody had spoken, Isidoro offered to decoy the Indians into the hands of the mutineers on condition that, in the event of his being successful, his own horses should be returned to him, and he should be allowed to go back to Sandy Point.

Isidoro was well known to most of the mutineers by reputation, as a man of great craft and adroitness, and as they had no doubt of his ability to be as good as his word, his offer was eagerly accepted. He then explained that in the first place it was necessary before maturing his plans, that he should reconnoitre the Indian camp, and in order not to arouse the suspicions of Riquelmes, he requested that two men should be sent to accompany him. Of these two, he had no doubt that he would be able to dispose in some way or other, as soon as he had got a safe distance from the main band, as, strange to say, his capturers had neglected to take his revolver from him. The rest of his escape he left to Providence and his good horse.

But Fate was willing to make matters easier for him than he anticipated. Riquelmes was completely taken in by this little artifice, and fearing lest the sight of the Chilians should awaken mistrust in the minds of the Indians, he suggested that Isidoro should go alone.

Five minutes afterwards Isidoro was leisurely cantering over the plain in the direction of the mysterious specks, to whose timely appearance he owed his sudden release. After he had gone about two miles, the plain was crossed by a deep cañon. Into this he descended, disappearing, of course, from view of the mutineers, who expected to see him shortly emerge again on the opposite side. How long they watched for his reappearance is neither here nor there, but after a certain lapse of time it no doubt gradually began to dawn upon them that they had been guilty of considerable simplicity, and that in all probability they would never see Isidoro again.

As for him, the moment he reached the bottom of the cañon, he clapped spurs to his horse, and followed its windings at breakneck speed till nightfall, and then, after a short rest, he rode up on the plain, and commenced travelling southwards again, so that by daybreak he was many miles behind the mutineers, and perfectly secure from any chance of being pursued. He was, of course, happy to escape with his life, but all his horses being lost, he was now a poor man; his prediction as to the unfortunate issue to his trip, which he had made on losing his whip in crossing the Santa Cruz, was thus strangely verified. It was providential, after all, that Guillaume and I had crossed the Gallegos when we did; for we should otherwise have doubtless been taken prisoners by the mutineers, together with Isidoro, and being *bouches inutiles*, they would probably have shot us.

The mutineers slowly worked their way northwards, their numbers being thinned by the fatal disputes, which were of frequent occurrence. The horseless stragglers, too, unable to keep up with the main body, gradually died off from starvation and exposure, and finally, in the month of February, an expedition sent to the Patagonian coast by the Argentine Government, captured all that remained of the band, in the persons of about forty half-starved wretches, who were found wandering about the country somewhere in the vicinity of Port Desire. They were taken up to Buenos Ayres, and some difficulty as to their extradition having arisen between the Chilian and the Argentine Governments, they are still in prison in that city. The most culpable of the band taken prisoners by the *Magellanes* were shot at Sandy Point, last March, and the others were condemned to various periods of penal servitude.

I was leaning over the bulwarks of the steamer which was bearing me rapidly out of the straits back to the noisy work-a-day world. I had come up on deck to have a last look at Patagonia, for we were nearing Cape Virgines, and should now soon lose sight of land altogether. Darkness was coming on apace, cold gusts of wind ploughed up the foaming water, and the clouded sky looked gloomy and threatening. The main-land, half shrouded in a thick white fog, frowned sullenly down upon us as we swept past, and the dull muffled roar of the sea on the stony beach, which at intervals struck dismally on my ear, sounded like a half-suppressed growl with which the genius of the solitudes I was now leaving bade me good speed.

"Well," said a friend at my elbow, "I suppose you would not care to go to Patagonia again?"

I glanced at the scene before me, and as certain unpleasant memories which it called forth passed through my mind, I answered, shuddering, and with decided emphasis, "By Jove, no!"

Perhaps, had the day been fine, the sea smooth, the sky cloudless and blue, and the green slopes of the main-land bright with cheering sunshine, my answer might not have been so uncompromisingly in the negative. Forgetting minor inconveniences, I might have remembered only the pleasant features of my sojourn in the pampas, the rough simplicity of my everyday life, the frank kindness of my unconventional companions, the delights of the chase, the glorious gallops over immensity, with the pure exhilarating air of the desert rushing into my lungs and making my whole being glow with intense animation, the cheerful gathering round the warm camp-fire after the day's hard work, the hearty supper, the fragrant pipe, and then the sweet sleep in the open air, with the stars shining into my dreams.

Also Available from Nonsuch Publishing

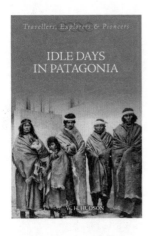

Written by the acclaimed novelist and naturalist William Henry Hudson, *Idle Days in Patagonia* is a detailed and unparalleled account of the kaleidoscopic wildlife of Patagonia, combined with lively anecdotes of Hudson's adventurous trips through the rugged and often inhospitable countryside.
£12
ISBN: 1-84588-024-2
160 pages, 27 illustrations

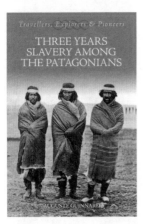

At the age of just 23 Auguste Guinnard was captured by Patagonian Indians and forced to live and work with them as their slave. *Three Years' Slavery* is a faithful record of Guinnard's brutal enslavement, surprising enlightenment and eventual escape and return to his homeland.
£12
ISBN: 1-84588-046-3
160 pages

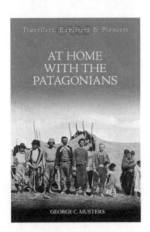

In 1869-70 George C. Musters spent a year living with the nomadic tribes of the Tehuelche in Patagonia. *At Home with the Patagonians* is a fascinating insight into a people and way of life so far removed from modern civilisation, yet in many ways remarkably similar.
£14
ISBN: 1-84588-008-0
256 pages, 10 illustrations